INVISIBLE ILLNESS,
VISIBLE
GOD

*When Pain Meets the Power
of an Indestructible Life*

~ 101 Devotions ~

MERRY MARINELLO

Hope Is My Anchor Publishing
Freeport, Illinois

Invisible Illness, Visible God:
When Pain Meets the Power of an Indestructible Life
101 Devotions

Copyright © 2013 by Merry Marinello.

All rights reserved. No portion of this book may be reproduced by any means, including duplicating, photocopying, electronic, mechanical, recording, the World Wide Web, email, or otherwise—except for brief quotation in printed reviews, without prior written permission from the publisher.

Published by
Hope Is My Anchor
www.hopeismyanchor.com

All scripture quotations, unless otherwise indicated, are taken from the Holy Bible, New International Version®, NIV®. Copyright ©1973, 1978, 1984, 2011 by Biblica, Inc.™ Used by permission of Zondervan. All rights reserved worldwide. www.zondervan.com

The "NIV" and "New International Version" are trademarks registered in the United States Patent and Trademark Office by Biblica, Inc.™

Scripture quotations marked (NASB) are taken from the New American Standard Bible®, Copyright © 1960, 1962, 1963, 1968, 1971, 1972, 1973, 1975, 1977, 1995 by The Lockman Foundation. Used by permission. www.Lockman.org

Scripture quotations marked (NLT) are taken from the Holy Bible, New Living Translation, copyright © 1996, 2004, 2007 by Tyndale House Foundation. Used by permission of Tyndale House Publishers, Inc., Carol Stream, Illinois 60188. All rights reserved. www.tyndale.com

Scripture quotations from THE MESSAGE. Copyright © by Eugene H. Peterson 1993, 1994, 1995, 1996, 2000, 2001, 2002. Used by permission of NavPress Publishing Group.

ISBN 978-0-9852603-2-3

For Dave,

From the beginning you believed in me and showed me with your words, action, and life the true and intimate love Christ has for us. No matter what limitation life has thrown at you, you continue to show me God is real, continue to inspire me to know him. I knew of God before. Now I see. Your sacrifice is not in vain.

And for Zachary and Anna,

Your father has given up many joys in this world, and you have had to as well; but God will redeem them all and more one day. Even so, life for now can be difficult and painful at times. But I know Dad would say his pain has been more than worth it if his testimony inspires you to know God more, if God uses his life to draw you near to Christ. Keep your eyes on Christ, and keep running the race. Your reward is not in this world. Thank you for walking this journey with us.

TABLE OF CONTENTS

ACKNOWLEDGEMENTS

It's been more than ten years since the Lord laid this book on my heart, and I am eternally grateful to all who have encouraged me to persevere in my faith as well as this endeavor.

Thanks to my family who put up with my absence when the writing muse captured me. You braved extra chores, nights I said, "Please get your own dinner," and other such sacrifices. Zach and Anna, your thoughts and questions inspire me, and Dave, you daily show me what love and selflessness look like.

Mom and Liz, you were my caregiver respite! Thank you for caring for Dave and the kids when I needed to get away.

Cliff Gilleland, Dick Burkett, and Justin Coverstone: through your ministry you have written a letter from Christ on the tablet of my heart, and will find much of that letter in these pages.

Thanks to Dawn Clark, Deborah Abbott, Lisa Woodward, and April Munson—each of you have shared your hearts and walked with me through the tears. Dawn, you have blessed us more times than I can count, and you lift me up when I am weary.

Every writer needs a good editor, and I was blessed with four: Justin Coverstone, Connie Fink, Donna Goeddaeus, and Marie Rippel. Thank you for helping me bring clarity to my sometimes scattered thoughts—Connie, your extensive notes were invaluable!

Scotty Rippel, you made my cover dream a reality! I'm so glad for your computer prowess.

I'm also grateful to Shelly Esser and Steve Demme for believing in our story, and to Ginger Kolbaba who inspired me to "Higher Goals."

Nickie Dumke, thanks for your practical help, inspiration, and encouragement over the years to pursue this project.

To Mike and Teri Vowell, our small group, and many friends at Park Hills who have cared and provided for our family: thank you for being the hands and feet of Jesus.

Friends at Grace—you show us what it means to be united with Christ and to keep going to the cross to feed our souls.

Candy Sanford—I couldn't have made it without you and the Lyme Caregivers group in those first years.

To the readers who remember when I first said I was writing this book, who have waited for it to come to fruition—thank you and may God bless you as you read this.

To those who have helped me in small and large ways, if I have neglected to mention you here, please forgive me.

And finally, thanks to the Lord who has carried us all these years. Thanks for sitting with me, and showing that you long to *reveal* yourself to us. May you continue to open our eyes. ℘

INTRODUCTION

The angel of the LORD came back a second time and touched him and said, "Get up and eat, for the journey is too much for you." So he got up and ate and drank. Strengthened by that food, he traveled forty days and forty nights until he reached Horeb, the mountain of God.

~ I Kings 19:7-8, NIV

"I've had enough Lord," Elijah said. "Take my life…"

With his heart pounding wildly and sweat streaming from his body, the man of God ran for more than 100 miles. Then he made a day's journey into the wilderness, collapsed under a broom tree, and asked to die.

It never seems like it at the time, but it's good that God doesn't answer all of our prayers the way we want him to.

Yet like Elijah, when we struggle with chronic illness we can also feel exhausted, terrified, as if we're running for our lives, trapped, alone, or that no one cares. Sensing no end in sight, we may also feel tempted to beg for any kind of ending we can get.

Jezebel, who threatened to kill Elijah, was certainly no match for God. Elijah had just seen God powerfully defeat false gods and destroy 450 prophets of Baal. And yet he ran.

Illness, crises, troubles of all kinds—we know these are also no match for God. He can easily solve them—or he can enable us to face our troubles with grace and strength. And yet…we run, too.

Sometimes we run because, for whatever reason, God has chosen not to remove our troubles. We run because suddenly we can't imagine living the kind of life that we find before us: no end in sight, trapped in illness or in the pain of seeing a loved one trapped in illness—and that pain on top of the pain of the circumstance overwhelms us. Like a burden too heavy to carry, it makes the journey too much.

That's the situation I found myself in. My husband and I had been married for eleven years, and spent several of those years looking for answers to his illness that likely started even before we were married. My husband's condition gradually worsened until the list of seemingly unrelated symptoms finally left him disabled and changed our lives forever. Eventually he was diagnosed with chronic Lyme disease. Our children were 1 and 3 then. Now they are teenagers and we persevere in the journey God has given us.

You may be told many times, by well-meaning friends, that God doesn't give us more than we can bear. I say, sometimes he does. The journey is too much, and we need food if we are to endure. The kind of food that can sustain us for a forty-day or forty-year journey into the wilderness—the kind of food that will enable us to seek the Lord as Elijah did.

I don't know what end is in sight for your fight with chronic illness, nor do I know what the future holds for my family's struggle. I do know that the Lord longs to reveal himself to us. God is near! I pray the scriptures in this book will be food for your soul as they have been to mine.

The sections can be read individually as devotionals, or together as chapters. Don't worry about "missing a day." Take time to meditate or journal as the Lord leads you.

May the Lord carry you when the journey is too much, when you are too weak to go on. Come to him and he will give you the *rest* you so desperately need—and the *vision* to see his hand in your life today. Come with me, and we'll walk together on this journey to see our Lord. ∞

Part One

WALKING WITHOUT SEEING
Suffering and Perseverance

*"The LORD gave
and the LORD has taken away;
may the name of the LORD be praised."*

~ Job 1:21

*"Shall we accept good from God
and not trouble?"*

~ Job 2:10

Chapter One

EYES THAT BEHOLD HIM
God, I Can't Go On!

I can see,
And that is why I can be happy,
In what you call the dark,
But which to me is golden.
I can see a God-made world,
Not a manmade world.[1]

~ Helen Keller

~ *Day 1* ~

"It happened again," my husband Dave said as he slowly removed his coat. He held the railing and painfully climbed the stairs, two-footing each step. Someone had rammed another shopping cart into him at the store.

Back then, Dave had no cane or wheel chair to alert people that sometimes his legs wouldn't move on command; his illness was invisible. Now, even with the cane, people still don't see.

But I see it every day, and sometimes the anger burns in my heart against God and man. *Don't they see? Doesn't God care?*

That day the rage rammed into my spirit until I too couldn't make it up the stairs—steep, long stairs to God, stairs full of fear, unending exhaustion, inadequacy. *I can't do it, God. I am empty, will you fill me? That's all I have for you.*

Are you also feeling empty? Are you running on fumes to get through the day as you wrestle with an invisible illness? You are not alone. Nearly one in two Americans (133 million) have an "invisible" chronic illness,[2] and nineteen million are severely disabled by something we don't see.[3]

Where are you, God—because you don't seem near. Why, God? This makes no sense. When will you heal? I can't live with this! "My God, my God, why have you forsaken me?"[4]

And there he is: our Savior who walked this road ahead of us and walks with us now as we echo his words from the cross. We will see him. He is beckoning us now, *come on a journey*. It's not an easy journey. It's not a fast journey. But we will not be alone.

> "You will seek me and find me
> when you seek me with all your heart.
> I will be found by you," declares the LORD...
>
> ~ Jeremiah 29:13-14a ❧

~ *Day 2* ~

Surely, O God, you have worn me out;
you have devastated my entire household...
My days have passed, my plans are shattered,
and so are the desires of my heart.

~ Job 17:11

My husband Dave was a children's pastor until the summer of 2000 when an undiagnosed illness left him unable to think clearly, remember names and job duties, or hold regular conversations. He had tremors in his arms and legs, and pain in joints and muscles. Sensitivities to light, sound, motion, chemicals, molds, and even cooking smells caused dizziness, headaches, or blackouts.

We had been to thirteen doctors in three years. I combed the Internet, researching everything from Chemical Sensitivities to Mad Cow Disease, while raising our toddler and preschooler.

In the movie *Chariots of Fire,* Olympic Sprinter Eric Liddell said, "I believe that God made me for a purpose. But he also made me fast, and when I run, I feel his pleasure."[5] Dave has a shepherd's heart, and when he ministered he felt God's pleasure like the runner's cool breeze. I could almost feel the wind—he was doing what God created him to do. Then one day our dreams died.

Many invisible illnesses take months or even years to diagnose. They can affect the young or old: 60% of those living with daily illness or pain are aged eighteen to sixty-four.[6]

Sometimes in the midst of trials and pain, we lose sight God and his character. We may find ourselves asking,

What kind of God allows intense pain
for seemingly no purpose?

How can we find comfort in his presence, or put confidence in his purpose for us? Job was honest with God—he poured out his heart. He wasn't afraid to say what he thought. Are your dreams shattered? Cry out to God. He is listening, even when you don't hear him.

I say to God my Rock, "Why have you forgotten me?..."
My bones suffer mortal agony as my foes taunt me,
saying to me all day long, "Where is your God?"
Why are you downcast, O my soul?
Why so disturbed within me?
Put your hope in God, for I will yet praise him,
my Savior and my God.

~Psalm 42:9-11 ❧

~ *Day 3* ~

How long, O LORD? Will you forget me forever?
How long will you hide your face from me?
How long must I wrestle with my thoughts
and every day have sorrow in my heart?
How long will my enemy triumph over me?

~ Psalm 13:1-2

"It doesn't seem like God loves Daddy very much since he won't heal him," my seven-year-old son Zachary asked, after four years of Dave's disability. "I thought God healed people quickly?"

At seven going on thirty, my son asked the question adults struggle to answer:

How can we trust the God who allows pain?

Sadly, the divorce rate among the chronically ill is over 75%.[7] And physical illness or uncontrollable physical pain is a major factor in 70% of suicides.[8] We always need God, but during an illness, that chronic need is brought sharply into focus.

One time soon after Dave was disabled, he left the house without telling me. Several hours later he finally called, unable to remember why he had gone out or how he'd gotten there.

Does he have Alzheimer's? I wondered. For weeks I hid the car keys until I knew he could drive safely again. But his physical lost-ness mirrored my spiritual confusion, the endless stream of questions, the searching and need for answers.

"Look on me and answer, O LORD my God.
Give light to my eyes, or I will sleep in death;
my enemy will say, 'I have overcome him,'
and my foes will rejoice when I fall."

~ Psalm 13:3-4

One day I met Jerry (not his real name) in a hospital cafeteria. He wrestled his tray to the table like a wildlife warrior grappling with a crocodile. His movements were quick, calculated to minimize agony. He sat down with a heavy sigh, adjusted his back brace, and wiped the sweat and furrows of pain from his brow.

People often misunderstood his needs—expecting slow movements instead of quick ones, thinking he would prefer the elevator over the stairs (but the elevator's jerking hurt his back more). Then at his darkest hour, his wife left him.

Had God left him too?

> But I trust in your unfailing love;
> my heart rejoices in your salvation.
> I will sing to the LORD,
> for he has been good to me.
>
> ~ Psalm 13:5-6

Where did the Psalmist find such strength, faith, courage in the midst of devastation? How can we, when we trusted the promises life held out to us, and now our dreams are crushed?

When we face trouble, we often find ourselves asking, *Why? How can I understand what God is doing?* Sometimes people answer this question by misusing Romans 8:28:

> And we know that in all things God works for the good of those who love him, who have been called according to his purpose.

God doesn't say that the terrible things that happen in our lives are good. He says that IN ALL things (good and bad) he is working for the good of those who love him. Who is this powerful God who can use the tragic, the painful, for good? Who are we, that God entrusts us with such a great expectation of our faith? God is seeking us and working for our good. Will we seek him? When life is devastating, will we trust him? ∞

~ *Day 4* ~

Why, O Lord, do you stand far off?
Why do you hide yourself in times of trouble?

~ Psalm 10:1

Nervously I stood at the edge of a cliff facing twenty high schoolers who egged me on. Dave and I were youth leaders on a rappelling trip (eight years before his disability), and I was in full gear, toes on the rocky ledge, heels about to step off.

"Now lean back," the instructor said; it was the most unnatural thing I could imagine. I lay down on a bed of air: cloudless sky my blanket, feet desperately seeking firm footing, body parallel to the ground. The view was incredible; blue sky and treetops embraced me, called me to look beyond myself.

My natural inclination was to let my feet reach toward the ground and allow my body to become upright—but if I let that happen, my body would crash into the rocks. It was not natural to keep my feet upon the rock, or to trust that I wouldn't plummet to the ground, but the harness held me fast. "And this is what it's like to trust God," we all marveled to each other. "He will hold us up when our feet stay on the Rock."

Have you heard God's encouragement? *Lean back—step off the cliff and trust.* It takes time to learn how to live on the precipice. It doesn't feel natural! The precipice can be a place of danger where we fight for survival, or a place of security, hope, and rest. This is God's daily calling, to lean back in him and trust.

I waited patiently for the Lord;
he turned to me and heard my cry.
He lifted me out of the slimy pit,
out of the mud and mire;
he set my feet on a rock
and gave me a firm place to stand.

~ Psalm 40:1-2 ∞

~ *Day 5* ~

> When God is the supreme hunger of your heart,
> he will be supreme in everything... And when you
> are most satisfied in him, he will be most glori-
> fied in you.[9]

> ~ John Piper

How can we get to this wonderful point of hungering for God, and being satisfied by him? It's easy to say, "Just trust God!" but it's hard to "lean back." Some days it's too painful. I find myself feeling lost, scrambling for my foothold, struggling to hold on to the precipice of life. I can hear God calling me to step off. *"I can't!"* I scream inside.

Then God in his mercy lifts us into the loving arms of Jesus, and offers us treasures from our suffering: perseverance, character, hope—the eyes that let us see God.

> ...And we rejoice in the hope of the glory of God.
> Not only so, but we also rejoice in our sufferings,
> because we know that suffering produces perse-
> verance; perseverance, character; and character,
> hope. And hope does not disappoint us, because
> God has poured out his love into our hearts by
> the Holy Spirit, whom he has given us.

> ~ Romans 5:2b-5

Perseverance is wrestling with, and eventually accepting God's sovereignty. It is understanding the full scope of the "fear of the Lord," the beginning of wisdom. The same sovereignty that brings us fear and anger also holds our hope for peace and comfort. Perseverance sees God in control.

Character is learning to apply perseverance. To strengthen that muscle that says "keep going!" To trust in God, not with a blind faith, but with a faith that sees the God who won't abandon us. Not a faith that has never doubted, but a faith that has wrestled with hard questions and comes out the other side insisting, I won't give up, I WILL see my God. A faith that hungers for the Lord.

Hope believes in God's glory—that something worthwhile will come from suffering. Hope fixes its eyes on the love of God that is poured into our hearts. Not a "someday by-and-by" love, nor the distant love of an uninvolved God, but the deep abiding love of a God who weeps when we weep. We draw near, and he satisfies.

The world insists we cannot be satisfied unless our circumstances meet our desires and expectations.

> It is the work and nature of unbelief to belittle and limit the fullness of Christ in the eye of the soul. It...conceals and locks up Christ's treasure and fullness...There is a rich, a glorious, and an overflowing fullness of all good treasured up in Christ for poor sinners, and his grace abundantly exceeds both our wants and sins.[10]
>
> ~Edward Pearse, c. 1673

But these three—perseverance, character, and hope—see a God who transcends our circumstances. They offer a view of God that is hard-earned through sweat and pain and tears. A view we otherwise wouldn't comprehend.

> "And after my skin has been destroyed,
> yet in my flesh I will see God,
> I myself will see him with my own eyes—
> I, and not another.
> How my heart yearns within me!"
>
> ~ Job 19:25-27 ⬛

Lean Back

Like my rappelling experience, God calls each one of us in our faith journey to *lean back*—to step off the cliff and trust. So often we seek the firm footing of trusting God *for* something, a specific answer, without which we doubt and mistrust him. But instead, God calls us to trust him *with* something—our hopes, our dreams, our needs and desires...with our very lives. To give that much trust, we need eyes to see him.

Do you wrestle as I do? I am not always able to see God. I don't even always want to see God! Life can seem like a dissonant harmony that hangs senseless in the air, lonely strains of music without direction, full of sorrow. But then God's love comes along and wraps me in his melody, and the music takes form—and it soothes my soul. Let him sing to you.

> "See, from his head, his hands, his feet,
> Sorrow and love flow mingled down:
> Did e'er such love and sorrow meet,
> Or thorns compose so rich a crown?" [11]
>
> ~ Isaac Watts

There are two lines of music that are richer together than apart, the melody and the harmony. Sorrow is like harmony. It makes little or no sense on its own. Only when "sorrow and love flow mingled down" does the harmony make sense. To rejoice is not to pretend life doesn't hurt, but to follow in the footsteps of Christ who considered a relationship with us a joy worth paying the price of great sorrow.

Maybe that price seems too great to you right now. I can understand that. I look ahead at the unknown, I hear my husband's cries of pain each day, I long for the intimacy we once had—and I long for God. God does not call us to be placated by a mere lesson in self-improvement. Knowledge is not a panacea. The pain is real, here, now—a raw and open wound. But the salve is here, now—God's real presence. His healing will continue longer than the wounds ever will, because God's love endures forever.

The "fullness of joy" is in God's presence (Psalm 16:11, NASB)— in intimacy with him, in seeking him, in pouring our hearts out to him and basking in Christ's over-abundant love for us.

In my deepest pain, I sometimes have no strength to go to God. But sometimes I listen to the story of someone else trusting God through their pain, and somehow their words lift me into Jesus' arms, and he carries me into the Father's presence. If you are feeling too weak to go to God, just say, "Help, God!" and read on. Perhaps as others have done for me, our experiences will lift you into Jesus' arms at a time when you are too weary to walk.

Let God speak to you now. He is calling to you, drawing you near, longing to spend time with you, waiting to be enjoyed like a cool summer day. He understands, and beckons us to lay back and breathe in the incredible view of our God. &

Chapter Two

CALL ME MARA
Where Is God When I'm Angry?

I cry aloud to the LORD;
I lift up my voice
to the LORD for mercy.
I pour out my complaint before him;
before him I tell my trouble.
When my spirit grows faint within me,
it is you who know my way.

~ Psalm 142:1-3a

~ *Day 6* ~

"Don't call me Naomi," she told them. "Call me Mara, because the Almighty has made my life very bitter. I went away full, but the LORD has brought me back empty. Why call me Naomi? The LORD has afflicted me; the Almighty has brought misfortune upon me,"

~ Ruth 1:20-21

"I know you want to believe there's something wrong with your husband, but there is absolutely no way he has Lyme disease," came the condescending tone of the neurologist on the phone. The words infuriated me. Why would someone "want" to think something was wrong with someone they love?

But as the doctor noted, nothing showed on the MRI, X-rays or EEG. It made no sense! *God, will we ever find out what's wrong?*

When a person is looking for a diagnosis, waiting for answers is agonizing. Strong emotions rush in. Depression, rage, resentment, horror, exhaustion, renewed resolve to fight and win—or despair and a feeling of final defeat.

What do we do with these strong emotions? Do we trust God with them? Or do we use them as shields to push God away?

Perhaps our earliest mentor in dealing with anger and pain is Job. "Night pierces my bones; my gnawing pains never rest." His breath was offensive to his wife, and he was loathsome to his own brothers, small children, and all of his friends. Job bravely declared: "Have pity on me, my friends, have pity, for the hand of God has struck me" (Job 30:17, 19:14, 17-19, 21).

In Job we can find the courage to be totally honest with God, to pour out anger and pain—and discover that God is big enough to bear the brunt of our bitterness and grief.

This is the truth Naomi expressed. "Call me Mara," she insisted when her husband and children died. Mara means *bitterness*. God made her life bitter, and she was willing to say so.

Naomi teaches us how to grieve. As she and Ruth walked together, so we are walking on our own journey. A journey to honesty, to no longer honey-coat our relationship with God but state in bold terms, as she did, that God does not only bring us blessings, but also trouble. It is a journey of walking in God's presence while our world is falling apart.

How can I love the One who makes me bitter?
How can I trust without knowing why he allows me to suffer?

Perhaps one reason we struggle with trusting God is that we want to trust him to give us the outcome *we* want. And right now, for whatever reason, he isn't doing it.

Instead we need to go back to the basics. Do we trust that God is who he says he is? That he really is working for our good when we can't see it? That he truly loves us? Are you willing to lower your shield of emotional pain and trust God to be your protection?

In the path where I walk
men have hidden a snare for me.
Look to my right and see;
no one is concerned for me.
I have no refuge; no one cares for my life.
I cry to you, O LORD;
I say, "You are my refuge,
my portion in the land of the living."

~ Psalm 142:3b-5 ☙

~ *Day 7* ~

> To say that we should pay no attention to pain because one day we shall be in heaven is to misunderstand both pain and heaven...To try to minimize present suffering on the basis of future hope is to rob both of them of their power to build character and accomplish God's purpose in this world.
>
> If, then, we don't eliminate or change suffering, we must be honest and either eliminate God or change our thinking about him.[12]
>
> ~ Warren W. Wiersbe

Most of us probably don't set out to change our assumptions about God. The journey we want is to change our circumstances—we want practical help and answers now! I remember thinking, "Dave has to get well; that's the only way we can continue on."

What does it mean to walk with God through suffering? Does it mean stuffing all pain deep inside, pretending to be strong because we have Christ? No! We must refuse to falsify our faith by pretense. God places in each of our hearts a longing for something real and true to cling to.

But can we really take our complaints to God? Remember the Israelites? They grumbled against God and Moses—and wandered in the desert for forty years because of it. Isn't God to be feared?

On the other hand, Job wasn't punished for asking God hard questions. Although God put Job in his place, he also honored Job before his friends. The difference? Job spoke rightly of God and his character; the Israelites turned their hearts back to Egypt and their souls to idols. They accused God of bringing them into the desert to die—contrary to his promise to them. They had the cloud by day and the pillar of fire by night—and yet they were blind to God and his purposes for them.

Are you ready to change how you think about God? Write down your assumptions about God, and leave some blank space underneath or on a facing page. Then ask God to open your eyes and show you who he really is. Come back to your notes over time, and write down what God reveals to you. Try to find scriptures that speak the same truths, and note those as well.

After you journal, take a few moments to just rest in our Savior's arms and know with your soul, he is your refuge.

Trust in him at all times, O people;
pour out your hearts to him,
for God is our refuge.

~ Psalm 62:8 ℘

~ *Day 8* ~

Why are you so far from saving me,
so far from the words of my groaning?
O my God, I cry out by day, but you do not answer,
by night, and am not silent.

~ Psalm 22:1b-2

Dave's memory came and went that first year. Every day he asked me if he had some place to go or a meeting to attend, and sometimes he packed his briefcase. Each time I reminded him that he no longer worked and that he was on medical leave. He would look blank, then surprised, then defeated. Sometimes he argued with me, or claimed I was joking. Slowly the realization would come back to him, he would remember—and my heart would rend. "That's right," he said slowly, with a weight in his words that matched the heaviness in his steps. "That's right."

Rejoice? How is that possible? I shouted in my mind. My husband is lost in confusion and I have nowhere to turn. I'm not joyful—call me Mara! My life is bitter. What joy is there in suffering or in perseverance? What is the hope that does not disappoint us?

We need to ask these questions, of ourselves, of each other, of God. They are important, vital to us beginning on our journey. Anger is often a good starting point because it is honest. If we don't tell God what's in our heart, we are lying.

Anger, disappointment, sorrow—these are not evils to be avoided but normal parts of the journey that offer points of decision. They are forks in the road. Will we take the road to bitterness—does anger rule us? Does sorrow become despair and hopelessness? Does disappointment become cynical? Or will we trust God and continue on the road, hungering for the only One who can satisfy?

At each point we have the choice, whether to put ourselves into God's hands no matter what, or to give in to bitterness. Bitterness and complacency are dead ends. But amazingly God continues to give us the choice. Even if we have given in to bitterness, it does not have to continue to rule over us. Bitterness blinds us, but we can choose to let go of it and look to God again.

We can walk with God no matter what emotions we have. Anger and sorrow are natural parts of the journey. It's how we respond to them that makes the difference in our path. When we honestly express our emotions to God, we come to a point where we can eventually pray,

God, none of this makes sense to me,
but somehow, be glorified. ❧

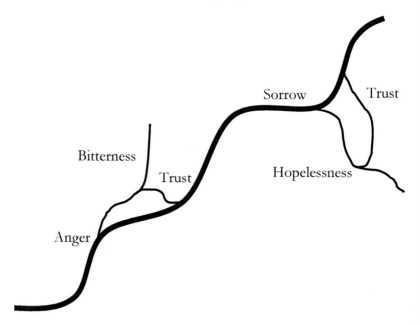

Forks in the Road

~ *Day 9* ~

> Consider it pure joy, my brothers and sisters, whenever you face trials of many kinds, because you know that the testing of your faith produces perseverance. Let perseverance finish its work so that you may be mature and complete, not lacking anything.
>
> —James 1:2-4

"Count it all joy" say James and Paul. I've often mused, *Where did God find these people? Are they for real?* Sometimes I find their words too much to bear, the road too difficult to walk.

Have you also wrestled with "rejoicing in our suffering?" Sometimes when people can see a reason for their pain, such as *it will make me a better person,* they are willing to accept it. But what if you have come to the end of yourself and can't see God's roadmap to character improvement? What if you are exhausted by mental, physical, or emotional pain? The carrot of becoming a better person can seem like a trivial reward—or even a knife in the back—when you're bleeding in the trenches.

When we head down the road towards bitterness and despair, Satan seizes the opportunity to skillfully aim several arrows at our hearts:

➢ Zing! Satan shoots: "I thought God promised to take care of you. Where is your God now?"

He never leaves us. Jesus said, "In this world you will have trouble" (John 16:33). I don't think many of us expect trouble, yet Jesus knew it was a certainty. God planned on it, do we?

➢ Zing! "You're so unworthy, why would God help you?"
➢ Zing! "God can never forgive you for what you did."

The Accuser leads us away from the hope and comfort of God, away from Christ's over-abundant grace. He leads us to mistakenly look at circumstances as a measure of our character instead of as a test of our character. Testing not to pronounce us failures, but to give us treasures that help us to draw near to God.

> ➤ Zing! "You served God and look how he repays you!"
> *"Maybe I can learn from this…"*
> "He's treating you worse than others!"

Satan sucks the joy out of James 1 and Romans 5 by appealing to our pride. Notice how easy it is to allow Satan to engage us in conversation, just as he did Eve.

> ➤ Zing! "God is punishing you."
> *"I don't know what for."*
> "Maybe God is not as just and loving as you thought."

We forget that Job suffered as a righteous man, and start to be blinded by Satan's arguments. It's easy to believe that health is a promise; that the use of our arms and legs, the ability to breathe normally, to eat whatever we want—that these things are owed to us by God. And when life doesn't turn out that way, we should rejoice? How could that be possible? Chuck Swindoll writes:

> …Joy is a choice. It is a matter of attitude that stems from one's confidence in God—that he is at work, that he is in full control, that he is in the midst of whatever has happened, is happening, and will happen.[13]

We don't feel that control when our health or the health of our loved one suddenly takes a turn for the worse.

The Father of Lies pours salt in our wounds, inflates our pride, and attacks God's character. And the arguments can sound so logical…but they are contrary to God's word. God has poured out his love into our hearts. He sought us while we were his enemies! While we were dead in sin—totally incapable of doing anything at all, Christ saved us. Now we are friends, brothers, dearly loved children, betrothed—God uses every close relationship we know to help us understand the depth of intimacy the Father-Son-Spirit holds out to us. And he calls us to a deeper level of trust.

But when our hearts are blinded by pain, it's hard to open our eyes to God's love. Why would we rejoice?

- ❖ He suffered before us. He understands.
- ❖ He suffered *for* us. We are *his*.
- ❖ He suffers *with* us. We are *united* with Christ. What happens to us, *happens to him*.

In suffering ourselves, we begin to understand the extent Christ went to, to rescue us. Pain is a window, and perseverance and character become eyes that let us see God through that window. Then we see how true it is that God pours out his love into our hearts. Then we begin to hope in the glory of God.

We may not be able to see how our circumstance can bring God glory, and some days it may be hard for us to care. Other days, this hope will encourage us that continuing on is worth it.

As we persevere, Jesus opens our eyes and we see the gift. Just like leaning back off the mountain, there is an incredible *view* to be had. Something that is far beyond a lesson to learn. A lesson can't feed us, cry with us. We can't lean back and trust in a lesson—we need something more, something that can fully carry our weight—we need God himself.

We will have pain in this life no matter what—that is a given. When we choose joy, we choose to walk through the pain of suffering to gain the eyes that behold our God. ℘

~ *Day 10* ~

> Therefore, I urge you brothers, in view of God's mercy, to offer your bodies as living sacrifices, holy and pleasing to God—this is your spiritual act of worship. Do not conform any longer to the pattern of this world, but be transformed by the renewing of your mind. Then you will be able to test and approve what God's will is—his good, pleasing and perfect will...
>
> ~ Romans 12:1-2

Some days I slip down memory lane, and remember the days when Dave worked at church—they seem so far away now. Echoing in my mind I hear, *"Grandma, this is our new pastor. He likes kids!"* This was high praise for Dave, coming from a sixth-grader who had just met him a few minutes before. Dave spent a lot of time with that sixth-grader, Steve, and the other junior high students. They used power tools together to build shelving, a cabinet to store puppets, and games for the kids' "carnival" nights. "If they build the games, they'll take better care of them—and of church property," Dave reasoned. He always had willing helpers to run the games for the little kids.

The boys were so excited. "We get to use those?" they asked in wonderment as Dave pulled out the drill and jigsaw. "Tools are loud and dirty, everything a boy could want!" Dave told me. He dovetailed his life into theirs with the skill of a pastor-craftsman. Their best products were not wood and paint, but character quality built over time and with loving workmanship.

That is the life we're supposed to be living, not this hellish roller-coaster of confusion and pain. God, this is insane! Why did you take it all away? Where is the man you gave to me? You let me have him for a glimpse, you taunt me with moments, and then steal him away again.

What about our lives didn't please you that you thought robbing this man—and the world—of Dave's joy to minister would somehow be better?

Do you hear the doubt, the unbelief in my thoughts? God robbed us, taunts us. God wasn't pleased with us. The pull of the road to bitterness is wide, strong, rational—and blind to God. And the treasures that God holds out to us in suffering are locked up tight. Where is the key to unlocking them?

Pastor Cliff, who counseled me the first three years of Dave's disability, handed me the key in Romans 12. "Be willing." Willing to go through whatever God puts in our path.

If life just happens to us, then we are victims. But God holds out to us a great honor. We are not victims if we lay down our lives, if we walk willingly with God on whatever path he has for us, even if that path is filled with pain that we can't escape.

When we lay down our lives, God is not our adversary, but our Leader who goes before us. He is the Friend who walks with us, the Father who lovingly carries the pieces of our broken hearts, the Beloved Bridegroom who suffers with us—and the Comforter who brings us peace.

> "And I will give you treasures
> hidden in the darkness—
> secret riches.
> I will do this so you may know
> that I am the LORD,
> the God of Israel,
> the one who calls you by name."
>
> ~Isaiah 45:3 (NLT) 🙠

~ *Day 11* ~

> Come to me, all you who are weary and bur-
> dened, and I will give you rest. Take my yoke
> upon you and learn from me, for I am gentle and
> humble in heart, and you will find rest for your
> souls. For my yoke is easy and my burden is
> light.
>
> ~ Matthew 11:28-30

When I was about to give birth to our oldest son Zach, I needed a new duffle bag for the hospital stay. My husband Dave came home with a monstrosity of a bag that could hold a year's supply of diapers! ("But it was on sale!" he offered.)

I'm a member of over-packers anonymous, so I dutifully filled that bag with all the things the "books" say you might want. A few changes of clothes, my nightgown, some toiletries, a robe, cd player and music. Some games, a camera, enough clothes for five babies (it was winter), the baby carrier, blankets, diapers, the childbirth books and magazines (like I could see to read during a contraction)...was I forgetting anything?

When we go on a journey, we choose what to pack. The type of journey determines what we pack. And in life, we get to carry whatever we pack, so pack light!

When we went to the hospital, I let Dave carry that bag. And Jesus is ready and willing to carry every person's oversized duffle bags of life's cares. We don't have the time or energy to carry around bags filled with bitterness; we need our energy for healing and caring for our loved ones.

We don't need clothes; God provides those in Christ. We need to put away the protective coverings we wear, the "shoulds" and the "ought-tos" that say we need to be perfect and never have negative thoughts. That's denial! Instead, we need to go ahead and express what we think to God. We carry too much weight when we try to contain our anger instead of allowing God to carry it.

When I started this journey, my suitcase was already packed full of ideas about God. I chose to dump it out and start over again. Jim Cymbala says "The first step in any spiritual awakening is demolition."[14]

I sought to unpack every thought except my willingness to relinquish myself to God. I thought I was willing to give my all until God came, asking for more. *I didn't sign up to be this kind of Christian! I signed up for the good life with maybe some minimal, obligatory ridicule.* But God is worthy of our all, even our suffering.

Don't carry anything God can carry. We can't carry tomorrow and its worries. These are the things we must unpack. Imagine the weight relieved to lay it all down, and to carry only a small key. Simple and light and yet of utmost value. He asks for our willingness to walk with the One who died for us, hand in hand, as he carries our heavy burdens, and we carry only this light and mysterious one. ∞

~ *Day 12* ~

"Shall we accept good from God, and not trouble?"
In all this, Job did not sin in what he said.

~ Job 2:10

When Dave was finally tested for Lyme disease, it was our last lead. His eyes were ringed with dark circles, as if he hadn't slept in weeks—in reality he slept 14-16 hours a day. We were escorted to a small, pristine white exam room where the proverbial pin drop sent waves of pain through my sound-sensitive husband's head. Anna, then eighteen months old, opened a cabinet door and it banged shut like a shotgun. Zach, three and a half, climbed onto the examination table, and the sound of paper crinkling reverberated like a jackhammer.

Finally the doctor came in, apologizing for being late. She opened Dave's inch-thick file, and showed us the results from two of his three Lyme tests. "They're both negative," she said. "I don't think you have Lyme. I'm sorry we haven't found the answer."

I don't remember what she said next. My mind went numb. Anna had begun crying when the doctor entered; now tears clouded my eyes and frustration clouded my judgment.

Dave was going to do some more blood work, and I decided to take the kids for a walk. I got the stroller out of the van and walked down the strip mall, unpacking as I went.

✓ *The really bad things only happen to other people—toss.*

✓ *God is nice and always protects you—toss.*

✓ *God doesn't let your world fall apart—toss.*

I feel empty and lost. I don't know who I am anymore, and I don't know who God is. Are you even real, God? Don't you care at all? Where are you?

I went back to the beginning of what I knew about God. God is sovereign. I had hit my head against that wall again.

Why, why couldn't this have been the answer for Dave? Just get it over with, God. I'm tired of all of this. I hate this!

Chuck Swindoll writes, "Some events hit with such ferocity they leave mental shrapnel embedded in our brains."[15] I felt those shards as I reviewed the doctor's words and the hopelessness of our situation. Then somehow amid this latest assault, I found the courage Job found, the courage to face God.

God, I can't take this anymore! You're God and yet you won't do anything! You won't lift a finger to make Dave better. Are you impotent?

But this time I was somehow willing to give that anger to God.

No, came the thought from within, *I know my God isn't impotent. He is all-powerful.* The battle raged on as I confronted my anger and struggled to remember the truth about God.

Are you callous, uncaring, sadistic?

No, I know my God is good, is loving.

Are you really not in control?

Yes he's in control; he is sovereign. Our situation neither surprises him nor thwarts his plans and purposes.

I was tired of the months of wrestling, fighting, demanding "justice NOW!" from God. I picked up my key, my willingness to walk with God, and fingered it with my mind, carefully examining the lock on my heart that God was somehow opening.

God this hurts so much, and I'm so angry with you for allowing it, but I submit my anger to you. You are sovereign; I am not. Have your way in my life. I feel like you are not all powerful, not all loving, not truly good, but I know those things are lies. My circumstances lie to me, they don't dictate the truths of your character. So I give it to you, God, and ask you to help me because I can't see my way past this one.

In my submission I could see that God is not an exacting God, expecting me to "hop to it!" and be happy that Dave is sick—he says be joyful always, but Romans 12:12 explains further: "Be joyful in hope, patient in affliction, faithful in prayer."

We are patient in affliction because we know it is only temporary—and because we now suffer *with* him. We understand more all the time how much he who suffered for us loves us. Patience does not rush in when we want it—it comes gradually over time, with trust, and with faithfulness in prayer. ❧

~ *Day 13* ~

Naked I came from my mother's womb,
and naked I will depart.
The LORD gave and the LORD has taken away;
may the name of the LORD be praised."
In all this, Job did not sin by charging God with wrongdoing.

~ Job 1:21-22

We all want prayer to change our circumstances, but sometimes God wants prayer to change us instead. Are we willing for God to have his way in our hearts if our problems are not resolved?

It is easy to think God is good and loving when the world goes our way, but when life gets hard, what do we believe? I have a friend who was told when her husband died, "Well, *someone* didn't have enough faith." Meaning her. To believe that because we have faith, God is obligated to do what we want, is arrogance and a twisting of his Word. It takes scriptures out of context, and is a very damaging heresy.

If we have faith, will God see the wisdom in our plans and do things our way?

Is the power in our prayers,
or is the power in the One to whom we pray?

How protected did Job feel? We like to remember that God is the refuge of the oppressed and the Father of the fatherless, but we forget that means there are people who are fatherless or oppressed.

My own father died from kidney disease when I was eight, after four long years of home dialysis. While God is my Father, he did not protect me from watching my father suffer and cry out in pain, or from being fatherless, or my mom from being a widow, or my grandmother from losing her son.

People don't want to say, "The Lord has taken away," as Naomi did. That doesn't sound very comforting. Perhaps you've been told lots of good-sounding, comfort-filled, trite sayings about God. The things you hear that are like daggers to the soul, the sayings that heap guilt on your faith, or rip open the wounds that are just starting a tenuous healing. They threaten to drive you farther away from God.

Sometimes your trial, your pain, doesn't just rock your world. It rocks others'. *What if God isn't who they think he is? What if God does something like this to them?*

We live in a sad world. God doesn't always heal. Tragedies happen. We don't understand. Is God still worthy of our praise?

We need to hear from someone who has lived through the valley, who knows the depth and breadth of trusting in God. Someone who *sincerely* praises God despite the pain. That is a person with a faith that moves the mountains of hurt in our hearts.

Paul, a man whose faith we could hardly doubt, looked at his thorn in the flesh as a "gift" from God, a way to see God's power.[16] In Hebrews 11 we learn that those of great faith persevered without receiving what was promised, and many were brutally martyred. Even Jesus found suffering and pain to be in the center of God's will for his life.

We need to unpack this idea that God won't let us suffer, and begin again. The reality is that we live in enemy-held territory—but what Satan plans for evil, God plans to use for good.
&

~ *Day 14* ~

Jacob called the place Peniel, saying, "It is because I saw God face to face, and yet my life was spared."

~ Genesis 32:30

We later learned that there can be false-negative tests and that there is quite a bit of controversy about how to diagnose Lyme disease.[17] Dave's third Lyme test came back positive. Although he never had the common bull's-eye rash, he did have a four-month flu-like illness years before we were married, which is characteristic of early Lyme. Because he had developed so many of the clinical signs and symptoms, he was diagnosed with chronic Lyme disease.

Do you wrestle with God as Jacob did? Do you long to see him—enough to not let go?

My friend Deborah wrote to me that she knows it is good to wrestle with scripture, but wonders if she is willing, as Jacob was when he wrestled with the angel,[18] to have her hip permanently dislocated out of its socket, and to gain a new name. A "name" to an Israelite held his identity. When Naomi asked to be called Mara, she was literally saying, "I am bitter, call me what I am."

Ironically as I wrestled, I found that admitting my mistrust of God was the beginning of my being able to trust him. I finally felt God had heard me, and then I was willing to listen to him. There was a new strength in our relationship. Before this it had been full of secrecy and lies though I hadn't realized it—but I had been trying to hide my true thoughts and feelings from God. No wonder I lived with an underlying level of insecurity.

When we agree to give God our anger in the midst of our suffering, we are engaging God in the contest of our wrestling.

If we bury or ignore our anger, we give up on God and ourselves. We have no hope of gaining a new name, enjoying the blessing of walking with God, finding peace in him, or finding rest in his sovereignty. We instead avoid spending time with God, and our anger grows and breeds.

Jacob wrestled in the dark, and we too wrestle in dark days, but eventually he saw God face to face. Don't let go of God until you see him. ☞

Lean Back

Have you ever expressed anger to God? Maybe you have but need to continue giving God your deepest anger.

Is your concept of God too small, as mine was? He is a big enough God to handle the likes of you and me! Your relationship with God will withstand your anger, because he truly is trustworthy. There is no condemnation for those in Christ.

If you have never trusted Jesus with your life, maybe now is the time to confess your sins, ask for forgiveness, and accept him as Lord and Savior of your life. He gave his life for you.

Is God calling you to unpack some of your thoughts about him, or to let him carry some unresolved emotions? Reach deep within the pocket of your mind and pull out your key. Ask yourself, "In my anger and pain, am I willing to submit to God? To be moldable, teachable? To find my peace in Jesus instead of in my circumstances?

Put down the burdens he is longing to carry. He waits with arms of grace, he loves you with an everlasting love, he has fought the spiritual battle for your soul—he treasures you.

If you don't know how to begin, pray with me:

God, open my eyes, show me a God I never expected to see. So many things blind me to your love and mercy: anger, fear, pain, frustration, lost dreams, bitterness, pride. Please forgive me, and help me to see your mercy and that your love endures forever. I give you my heart's desire and every part of my life; you may do with me what you want. It hurts sometimes; I'm blind and afraid. Show me the way to your peace, to that place where your love meets me at my deepest pain and restores my name, my identity, as you did Naomi's. Help me to rest in Jesus' arms. Amen. ☙

Chapter Three

ECHOES OF RAMAH
Sounds of Pain

A voice is heard in Ramah,
weeping and great mourning,
Rachel weeping for her children
and refusing to be comforted,
because they are no more.

~ Matthew 2:18

~ *Day 15* ~

The weapons we fight with are not the weapons of the world. On the contrary, they have divine power to demolish strongholds. We demolish arguments and every pretension that sets itself up against the knowledge of God, and we take captive every thought to make it obedient to Christ.

–2 Corinthians 10:4-5

"Daddy is very sick," our three year-old son Zach stated matter-of-factly from the back seat. Dave was on medical leave, but we didn't know what was wrong. So, we went camping for the week while a mold problem was fixed in our home.

"Am I very sick?" Dave asked me. He couldn't remember what was happening.

"We're doing everything we can to help you get better," I answered, trying to skirt the issue.

We were quiet for a few moments and then Dave asked, "Am I dying?"

"I don't think so."

Pause. "Is that the truth?"

"It's all I know."

I didn't know how to answer Dave's questions. I didn't know what would happen or how we would make ends meet. Life was changing so fast. Some days I woke up wondering if Dave would.

The question nagged at me—was Dave dying? What would I do? What if our baby Anna forgot Dave? No! Just the thought infuriated me. I could never allow that to happen.

I couldn't stop the thoughts coming: *Is it too late for Dave? Why did he go downhill so fast? What will I do without my soul-mate?*

I found myself getting angry over silly things—Zach not drinking his juice, Dave for being depressed. What was left of the Dave I married? Later that night I cradled his head in my arms and sang to him while we both cried.

Thoughts, questions, doubts and fears plague all of us when we face serious situations. The mind, even more than physical circumstances, is the real battlefield. What do we do with these overwhelming worries? How do we arrest these thoughts that keep marching in, worries that are not one bit concerned about our efforts to dispel them?

Two weeks before Dave went on medical leave, he gave one of his best sermons ever, on how to take every thought captive in Christ. He gave a visual picture of Masada, a mountain with steep sides and a flat top, where Herod the Great built a palace and stronghold. Roman Soldiers surrounded it in AD 73 to starve out the Jewish Zealots who were rebelling against the Roman government and taking refuge there. When we take our thoughts captive we surround them with truth and starve our negative thought processes until the thoughts die out.

It's hard to starve out fears and doubts when you don't know what you are facing. Debts skyrocket—are you facing bankruptcy? Marital problems—are you facing divorce? Chronic illness—are you facing death? Or perhaps even more frightening, a lifetime of physical and emotional agony?

Facing the unknown is something we do every day, but we only seem to notice it when the unexpected happens. Then suddenly the reality that we are not in ultimate control of our lives slaps us in the face. We wake up and wonder, *where is God?*

Wondering can become the lies: *he isn't here. He doesn't care.* And we must surround these lies with truth.

The truth is, God is always with us—through the good times when we perhaps take him for granted—and through the tough times. His promise is always sure:

> God has said, "Never will I leave you;
> never will I forsake you."
> ~ Hebrews 13:5b

~ *Day 16* ~

Jesus answered, "The work of God is this:
to believe in the one he has sent."

~ John 6:29

Dave's sensitivities to chemicals and smells added a growing list of rules to our lives. *Don't run the dishwasher while Dave is awake. No scented soaps, make-up, shampoo, deodorant, toiletries or cleaning supplies. Read all labels because 'Masking Fragrance' is a perfume in many 'unscented' products.*

Don't cook in the oven, or use spices, or pre-made sauces. I started using the crock pot in the garage, the bread maker in the far-removed guest bedroom, the coffee pot on the back patio, and the microwave instead of the stove whenever possible.

When we decided to go camping, I thought rest would help Dave get better—he'd be back to work by the end of the summer, right? Instead his memory and ability to think clearly dwindled.

Only when Dave and the kids slept did I feel I could truly let down my guard. Then I enjoyed the soft wind rustling nearby leaves while copying large portions of Job into my journal and questioning God. My journal was a refuge—it brought my fears to the surface, for God and me to face, surround, and starve.

This idea of taking every thought captive does not mean stuffing our thoughts. You can't face a fear that is buried—it's only when we bring those deep down doubts to the surface that we can face them and be relieved of their control over us. When we stuff our fears, we protect them, and feed them the resources they need to stay alive and active.

When Dave went on medical leave, we both feared the future. We felt so spiritually lost—as lost as Dave felt when he couldn't find his way home. He asked our pastor, "What do I do now?"

"Your job is to hang onto your faith," Pastor Cliff said. Those words, and the nobility of this work still resound in my mind. They remind me to seek the truth that disarms the power of my fears.

This is full-time, important, valuable work. The Christian world may weigh you down with added expectations. Let them go. Rest in the simple, profound work he has given. ∞

~ *Day 17* ~

"Since no man knows the future, who can tell him
what is to come? No man has power over the
wind to contain it; so no one has power over the
day of his death."

~ Ecclesiastes 8:7-8a

Near the end of that first summer, we sat in yet another
waiting room for yet another test (this time an MRI). Our children were playing at a friend's house. I couldn't remember how
many people had watched them while we went to doctors. This
was not how I had envisioned our married life.

On the way to the hospital, Dave had asked me what I was
thinking about, so I told him all the things God had been telling
me during my quiet time and how I was growing and changing.
How I was learning to rely on God and not my circumstances,
though I desperately wanted circumstances I could rely on.

Then I asked what he was thinking and he said, "The grass
is green. It's a nice green." Then he added sadly, "I don't have
deep thoughts anymore." These were not the words of someone who didn't want to be intimate; he did, and he compre-
hended his loss. That he knew he wasn't thinking right was the
hardest for me to take in. My husband with the master's degree.
My husband who in the early years had been the one to draw
me out. It would have seemed easier if he wasn't aware.

Reality was beginning to surface for me. The truth of the
unknown we were facing and the dawning of its seriousness
became clear.

Some parts of life cannot be sugar coated. Sometimes the
grass is not green. It's okay to admit that. And when it's the
truth, admitting it is a necessary step to starving out untruth.

Perhaps you know someone whose definition of encouragement means that something positive will erase all negative emotions. Yet if the positive denies the negative truth, it has no power to heal.

"Trust in the Lord," we tell someone who is struggling through a crisis, but what does that look like? Should we trust that God will choose to heal a man like Dave because he's a pastor? A child of God? A righteous man? Men like this die every day. Or perhaps the sufferer is a modern day Job? And after a time of suffering at Satan's hand, he will be restored?

We can look back after a trial and say such things, but not in the midst of one. We can trust in the character of God, but not what circumstances God will bring about. "No man knows the future…"

To take our thoughts captive, we need more than positive thinking. We need to confront the reality of our situation, no matter how awful and impossible—with the reality of our loving and sovereign God. As Robert S. McGee says, we need to "learn to master the process of tracing painful emotions back to their root false beliefs and replacing them with God's Word."[19] As deep as our pain reaches, his love reaches deeper.

So how can we do this? Several years ago, a counselor had me write down all of my negative thoughts. (I don't know if he knew just how prolific I would be!).

At first I thought it was a terrible assignment—why have someone who's hurting focus on all that negative stuff? (Did I mention I had a lot to write?). Didn't this process just give all those negative thoughts more power?

Then we began confronting the lies in my thoughts with truth. Many of my negative thoughts were worries—I was carrying the burdens of things that had not, and likely would not, happen. Many were subtle lies about God's character or his view of me that I didn't even recognize as lies until the thoughts were confronted with the truth of scripture. Soon I made up my own "Truth and Lies" chart that I could read when those thoughts crept in. Lies such as:

Lie: God abandons us when we're hurting

Truth: The Lord is close to the brokenhearted and saves those who are crushed in spirit. —Psalm 34:18

Lie: God is harsh and demanding

Truth: "He tends his flock like a shepherd: he gathers the lambs in his arms and carries them close to his heart; he gently leads those that have young." —Isaiah 40:11

Lie: I am unworthy of God's touch and love.

Truth: He quiets me with his love—Zephaniah 3:17
The one the Lord loves rests between his shoulders— Deuteronomy 33:11

God gives us freedom from the errors and lies in our thinking that add unnecessary weight to our burdens. We need to root them out with the truth.

> Jesus said, "If you hold to my teaching, you are really my disciples. Then you will know the truth, and the truth will set you free."
>
> ~ John 8:31-32 ක

See Appendix A for more *Truth and Lies*

~ *Day 18* ~

Why do you hide your face
and consider me your enemy?
Will you torment a windblown leaf?
Will you chase after dry chaff?

~ Job 13:24-25

The hospital was running two hours behind, and Dave kept forgetting why we were there, and asking if we could leave. An eight-year-old girl was playing while her mother had her MRI. Dave stared into space, his face devoid of expression, and it was all I could do to keep from crying. Where had my Dave gone? My Dave couldn't resist children. A child was an invitation to play, to interact, and to share the joy of being together. My Dave would have talked, comforted, distracted her while her mother was away.

What's life like for that mom? I wondered. *How discouraging for her that she has to come here alone, no one to stay with her daughter while she does the test.* But I don't have Dave's gregarious gift with people, and sometimes I don't know what to say. I open my mouth but no words come out. I feel dumb and incompetent and incomplete. I am less myself without my Dave, and the world is only half a world when he isn't there.

The man who once loved to serve and know people was now floundering like a swimmer needing to be rescued. Like many people with invisible illnesses, his symptoms were unpredictable. One day Dave might be able to go to several stores, the next he might not have the strength to leave the upstairs of our house. One hour he could forget what season it is and ask why there are leaves on the trees in winter, and the next he could remember detailed historical facts. I felt like I was drowning as well. The brief episodes when he was clear were only a gasp of air to me, a struggle to grab onto a life preserver that didn't exist.

I began to resent that as a pastor's wife I had given up simple joys like sitting together in church. Now I could sit with him at home, only it was like he wasn't really there. I could lean my head on him, but instead of comforting, my touches increased his pain.

I never thought about God "owing" us anything, but I had an unconscious expectation of protection from something like this. I resented God for allowing this to happen. We had served God in good faith! Just like Jacob from the Bible: he served Laban seven years to earn Rachel's hand in marriage, only to be tricked into marrying Leah. He had to work seven more years for Rachel. Was our situation God's idea of the bait and switch? But that wasn't consistent with my understanding of God. More insidious lies.

God is the one who "remembered" us as he had Rachel, when he opened her womb (Genesis 30:22). It's still miraculous to me how we longed and labored in our hearts for our son Zach for eight years, yet Anna was given so easily, without the heartache of empty arms. The name Zachary means "the Lord Remembers." Zach is my living reminder that God is always with us, that he listens and answers, that he remembers us with favor. *God, how can I reconcile these thoughts? Where are you? Why do you let this go on?*

We may wonder, *Is God really with me if he doesn't heal me or my loved one? What does trusting God mean?*

We learn to trust the God of the unexpected when we allow our despair to remind us of our need for God. We can turn to the God who understands and is waiting for us to lay all our trouble at his feet. And slowly we starve out despair as we replace it with the truth of God's character. ∞

~ *Day 19* ~

A voice is heard in Ramah,
weeping and great mourning,
Rachel weeping for her children
and refusing to be comforted,
because they are no more.

~ Matthew 2:18

The mother and daughter left, and Dave finally had his MRI that day. Part of me almost hoped for a brain tumor or an aneurysm, something that would be concrete and hopefully treatable. But nothing abnormal was found.

I sat for the quiet, long hour and waited, almost hearing the echoes of Rachel, weeping for her children. Voices of children who miss Dave and the voice of my own lost and hopeless dreams—weeping for my children. To Rachel's is added the voice of the nine year-old girl, playing by herself in the hospital waiting room. Another is heard, the prayers of young Emily, calling out to God every night because her pastor whom she loved is no more. Will he be healed?

And then echoes of Steve and other junior high and high school students, going into adulthood without the guidance they once enjoyed, stolen by an invisible foe. *"This is our new pastor. He likes kids!"* The tools they shared are quiet now, dusty on our garage shelf.

Who will cry out for the children who miss Dave, and for my own children who could not yet speak for themselves? I find, like Rachel, that I wonder *why should I be comforted?* To be comforted is to silence the voices, be untrue to my husband, to lie to the world, and eventually to defraud God's character. God cannot meet us in a pain denied.

I mourned the dream of our lives together, of the husband I loved and the father I longed for my children to know. When

Dave would black out, Zach tried to guess that Daddy was "sleeping" or "praying." He would try to understand what was incomprehensible even to me.

How should I pray for my children? "They need their father!" I told God, but I wondered if he agreed—that same God told me when I was eight that I would be okay without mine. I remember hearing Dad's screams of pain as I often hear Dave's now.

The tears came unchecked, refusing to be comforted by words devoid of power and meaning in their futile offer of hope. *If only I knew that Dave would be restored to me, I could cling to such a hope. If only I knew he would die soon, and then the great promise would be fulfilled for Dave that, "He who began a good work in you will carry it on to completion," and pain could be put to rest.* Instead I waited with empty arms, as a woman longing for a child, for the Lord to remember us, not knowing what form my hope would take.

The Lord is close to the brokenhearted
and saves those who are crushed in spirit.

~ Ps 34:18 ✆

Lean Back

Are you also waiting with empty arms? Are your feet struggling to find that foothold as you dangle off the precipice? Have you trusted God with your pain? I know it's not easy—but I also know that he will meet you in your pain if you allow him to. Read through the *Truth and Lies Chart* in Appendix A, and consider making your own chart.

One way to recognize the lies is to ask this question:

Do my thoughts magnify problems
or do they magnify the Lord?

Lies make problems bigger than they are. Truth sheds light on how big God is. Ask God to open your eyes to his truth.

You don't have to go to God alone, either. Go with a counselor, a pastor, a trusted friend, or a spouse when you open those precious places long sealed off from yourself and God. I didn't go it alone—my pastor, counselor, and several friends each played a different role in helping me to walk with God and hang onto my faith.

Maybe your pain is not from illness, but a past or present abusive situation. Again I urge you, don't be afraid to seek help.

Trusting God and emotional healing may take time—even years. Give yourself that time, take small steps. God is patient with us, and always watching for you—you are precious to him. You are his "handiwork" (Ephesians 2:10); the actual word is *"poema,"* his poem. He *remembers* you, calls you by name.

Lean back and lay your head to rest between his shoulders. Bring him the lies that threaten to rip our faith to shreds and let him quiet you with his love. The sounds of pain are terrifying, but the Shepherd's voice calls to us as the One who weeps with us and yet cares for us and protects us. ❧

Chapter Four

SITTING IN SILENCE
The Voice of God's Love

*Job's three friends…sat on the ground with him
for seven days and seven nights. No one said a
word to him, because they saw how great his suffering was.*

~ Job 2:11-13

~ *Day 20* ~

> My dear brothers, take note of this: Everyone should be quick to listen, slow to speak and slow to become angry, for man's anger does not bring about the righteous life that God desires.

> ~ James 1:19-20

One of the most aggressive treatments for chronic Lyme disease is IV antibiotics. The IV causes a Jarrisch Herxheimer or "herx" reaction as antibiotics kill off Lyme and release toxins in the bloodstream. I knew Dave would feel worse, but nothing prepared me for the confusion, the pain, the hallucinations—or the anger I would feel as life spun further out of control.

Soon I was mad at everyone and everything. I was ready for a fight. This big monster was against us and I fought it with everything I had, yet still came up short. Lyme was not going to be easily conquered. So unconsciously I looked for another adversary, a more manageable foe.

"God will carry you through," people said, "Just trust him." *Trust him? Look where God has brought us so far! What do you know about trusting God?* I should have asked, but I was too busy being angry. I might have learned something…or they might have.

"God will provide for you," another person offered as if dipping a sacrificial toe of encouragement in an icy pool of doubt. *Will he? What is God really obligated to do? I used to think that but now I don't know what God has promised me, and I think you question as much as I do when you look at us.*

"The good days help make the bad bearable," from someone who was never there to see firsthand. *No, they really don't!* I wanted to snap, but I smiled instead and felt incredibly alone.

Why do we want to look on the bright side to the extent that we invalidate pain? What is it we're afraid we'll learn? We are fragile people clinging desperately to our God who would never allow pain, but here he is, doing just that. What does he want, and why doesn't he think the way we do?

We hope for God to swoop down and rescue us from what this world has to offer so we don't have to learn firsthand that this life is closer to hell than heaven.

I was angry at the trite words, but sometimes I allowed anger to consume me. Dave's illness unlocked such ugliness in me. Suddenly I felt envy, hatred, fits of rage—where did they come from? I fought to go back and yield my heart to God again.

Self said, *"The world owes me for what we've gone through!"* Yet no one could give what I really wanted—my husband, our "normal" lives back—people couldn't give. They tried, but fell short, with their words.

As long as I was angry, there was nothing that anyone could say that would be right. It was always too trite, too aloof, too fake, too true, too spiritual, or too shallow—too sympathetic or too much walking on eggshells. I had to learn to forgive.

To *"mourn with those who mourn"* (Romans 12:15) is very difficult for us. "Comfort" seems more pleasant. It has a sense of resolution; good has been done. But what the suffering person needs is true comfort— someone to walk with them in the pain. Not someone to feel sorry for them or pity them—someone who will carry the pain as if it is their own.

People aren't going to say the right thing. They're going to fumble for words and make us angry. We can't control what people say, but we can control our reactions. Do we really want to carry anger and endlessly rehash words in our minds? Do we want to give people power over our lives that only God should have? It's hard to hear God through all that noise. Here again I found something worth unpacking.

> Bear with each other and forgive whatever grievances you may have against one another. Forgive as the Lord forgave you.
>
> ~ Colossians 3:13 ∞

~ *Day 21* ~

I will say of the LORD,
"He is my refuge and my fortress,
my God, in whom I trust."

~ Psalm 91:2

Dave was lonely. Our family lived hours away, and we had only lived here for two years. In that time Anna had been born and Dave had become increasingly sick; he hadn't had much energy after work for making friends.

Of his four closest friends, three moved away and a fourth also had a lot of health issues. *"How can I suddenly manufacture friends for Dave?"* I agonized. People were afraid to visit because of his chemical sensitivities.

Dave sat in silence, alone, for seemingly unending hours—a disquieting, disturbing, silence. Lyme alienated him from others, and I felt helpless to change that, though I often tried to get people to visit. For a while someone would visit him weekly or monthly, but then the visits would die out. Sometimes it was months in between visits from others.

There were a few who didn't forget him, and they were like jewels to me. Simple things like a card, a call, or a visit were like a candle in a window on a dark night saying, "he's not forgotten."

What do we do with these offenses? People say the wrong things, avoid us, abandon us—shall we carry around the bitterness? Allow the power of pain to eclipse the joys that come our way when someone does remember us?

On top of that, I felt as though I betrayed Dave by my own humanity. I betrayed him each time I walked out the door to do something normal, to visit friends, to escape the reality he could never escape.

Thankfully a dear friend reminded me that to never leave home was unrealistic! Caregivers are notorious for neglecting themselves. Please take care of yourself. The checklist in Appendix B will help you get started.

But the feelings often lied to me, taunted me. Was I rejecting Dave by sometimes wanting to get away from him? It was hard as a caregiver to not feel totally responsible, but I had to forgive myself for "failing" him when I left him alone.

If I can forgive myself—then surely I can forgive others too. I'm really not so different from them; I too avoid uncomfortable situations. Would I also avoid Dave if he wasn't my husband? I can forgive—but I can also change and learn not to avoid hurting people.

Forgiveness is a big part of letting go, of facing our anger instead of stuffing it. Anger doesn't have to control us; we have a choice to make.

As I worked through my thoughts and emotions, I was shocked to discover that I was angry with Dave. *Why did he get sick, why didn't he realize all these years what was happening to him? Why did he always have to be so strong, to fight back so that no one knew what he was battling—and now it's too late! Why did he abandon me?*

I was angry with myself for being angry at Dave. He hadn't done anything on purpose, but I had to let the anger out. I had to learn to forgive him his humanity, and hope that he could forgive me mine.

Perhaps most shocking of all, I found I had to forgive God. That sounds so strange—God isn't wrong! But our perception of him often is. And oh, how we misjudge his love, how shallow our perception is compared to the reality!

All these "voices" we hear from others and our own thoughts make people—and even God—seem distant and uncaring. We feel isolated, misunderstood, abandoned. Suffering leaves a gaping, God-sized wound, and I had to wait—and trust—for him to heal it.

God, I'm still angry with you. How can I give that over? I thought it was gone, and here this anger has surfaced again.

Dave's suffering has repeatedly taken me to a deeper level of surrender than I am used to, it is an intense spiritual battle. Sometimes all I have is a blind sense to hang on, that somehow God is worth it.

But sometimes I hear a deeper voice:

"As the Father has loved me,
so I have loved you."
~John 15:9

"Greater love has no one than this—
that he lay down his life for his friends."
~John 15:13.

Jesus loves you as much, and in the same way, as the Father loves him. How can we even begin to fathom how intimately he knows us, how tenderly he carries us through these painful times and always?

"...I am in my Father, and you are in me,
and I am in you."
~John 14:20.

United. Forever and inextricably. We are not abandoned—we are cherished by the One who has pledged his undying love to us, who goes through every hurt with us, who knows even more than we do the wrenching pain of laying down one's life—and he did that to be with us forever.

~ *Day 22* ~

And my God will meet all your needs
according to his glorious riches in Christ Jesus.
~ Philippians 4:19

Finances didn't worry me—at first. Surely Dave would be better soon. Dave's salary was still coming in, and we had some emergency savings. But as those early weeks turned into months, the truth began to sink in: Dave was facing long-term disability.

I dreaded the day when Dave's disability insurance would be approved. The church had agreed to pay Dave's salary until disability started, and then on that day our income would go from 100% to 60%. Meanwhile our medical costs exceeded our mortgage payments...

A 40% pay cut! Can we really live on this? What can I sell—my violin, our furniture, books, music... Suddenly we don't need much. Maybe the house? No! I remember house-hunting with Dave, his headaches and passing out from damp, moldy basements—our house is the one safe place in Dave's life.

Should I get a job? I'd have to put the kids in daycare; who would take care of Dave? I'd never forgive myself if something happened to him, or the kids. God, I'm so lost!

The day I received the letter from the disability insurance informing us of Dave's limited coverage, I also got a call from Pastor Cliff.

"The disability came through," I told him.

"That's great!" *Yeah great. It's a sock in the gut!* Then Cliff continued, "The elders are going to recommend that the church continue Dave's salary through the end of the year, and your family's health insurance beyond that time."

I sat down, speechless. The noise of my worries had over-whelmed me earlier. Frantic with fear, I had imagined the house in shambles with everything sold, but with a few words the house was back in order and my courage was renewed.

God doesn't owe me anything, he doesn't have to rescue me—and yet at my weakest hour, when I least deserve it, here he is again. I am humbled. God, you soften my heart with your love.

He reached down from on high and took hold of me;
he drew me out of deep waters.
He rescued me from my powerful enemy...

~ Psalm 18:16-17a

Anxiety, fear, worry, hopelessness, inadequacy, feelings of worthlessness, anger.... What name does your enemy go by? The One we lean back on, the One who keeps us from crashing to the ground, rescues us.

That rescue may not always look like what we want it to. One family might get the healing longed for; another might lose the house. We can look at each other and say it's not fair—and this, too, is the voice of our enemy. Or we can ask God to open our ears so that we truly hear him instead.

"Does he not leave the ninety-nine...and go after the lost sheep?...And when he finds it, he joyfully puts it on his shoulders..." (Luke 15:4-5)

He *joyfully* carries you; he *knows* your name.

"The hired hand...when he sees the wolf coming, he abandons the sheep and runs away" (John 10:12). But the good shepherd "lays down his life for the sheep. I know my sheep and my sheep know me—just as the Father knows me and I know the Father" (John 10:14 & 15).

He knows you just as he and the Father know each other. His intentions and promises to you are sure. ∞

~ *Day 23* ~

"Remember those in prison as if you were their fellow prisoners, and those who are mistreated as if you yourselves were suffering."

~ Hebrews 13:3

Some people I knew online struggled for two or three years to get Social Security Disability. We were fortunate that Dave's work provided disability insurance to support us in the interim.

Social Security Disability coverage, once approved, starts five months after the onset of disability. I often wondered, *do most people have five or six months—or two to three years—of living expenses in their savings?*

One day in the Social Security office, I overheard a man ask, "What do I do for food and insurance? How do I take care of my family?" His questions haunted me.

"What will we do, God?" I wanted a miracle that would end Dave's suffering and solve all of our problems. God brought me a different one than I expected. God spoke to me from Matthew 6.

"Look at the birds of the air,"
"They do not sow or reap or store away in barns,
and yet your heavenly Father feeds them.
Are you not much more valuable than they?"

The first fall Dave was on medical leave, cooking smells made him pass out, or gave him headaches that made him leave the house. One day a woman from church said, "I'm going to coordinate meals for you. How many times a week would you like them?" They brought meals for four months.

"Who of you by worrying can add a single hour to his life?"

The church paid Dave's salary and benefits for seven months, and medical insurance for two years.

> *"See how the lilies of the field grow?*
> *They do not labor or spin..."*

One man insisted, "You call me if you need tires or repairs for your car." Friends gave us food, clothing, and gift certificates at various times. Sometimes money came anonymously.

> *"Do not store up for yourselves treasures on earth...*
> *but store up for yourselves treasures in heaven...*
> *for where your treasure is, there your heart will be also."*

The Sunday school and AWANA children created dozens of cards for Dave. A little boy wrote, "Get better sune. I hope you fell better." Another drew a heart between two smiley faces. Their rainbows and birds and flowers and crosses decorated our home and our hearts. They opened our eyes to God's treasure.

> *"The eye is the lamp of the body. If your eyes are good,*
> *your whole body will be full of light. But if your eyes are bad, your*
> *whole body will be full of darkness..."*

Neighbors shoveled our walk, the youth group fixed a kids' fort that a family donated, and others did household repairs.

I began to realize how incredibly blessed we were, what a unique and beautiful gift the body of Christ is supposed to be. God in his mercy met our needs through the people around us.

> *"Therefore do not worry about tomorrow,*
> *for tomorrow will worry about itself.*
> *Each day has enough trouble of its own."*

> ~ *Matthew 6:25-34* ❧

~ *Day 24* ~

"But if we have food and clothing,
we will be content with that...
Godliness with contentment is great gain..."

~ 1 Timothy 6:8, 6

One Sunday a friend said, "God has laid it on my heart to watch your kids this week." The next day, Dave's new doctor called to offer an appointment weeks earlier. This doctor was a ten-hour drive away and it meant leaving the kids for 3 days. I marveled at how God provided for our kids before we knew we had a need.

"Trust God to meet your needs," Pastor Cliff encouraged me.

"But God doesn't define needs the same way I do!" I argued. *My children need a healthy father. I need to know how we will live. I don't want "daily bread," I want tomorrow's manna today!*

"That's right," he said, "we must trust him both to define and meet our needs." That thought was transforming for me. If God didn't answer what I thought I needed, I began to say, "Okay, God, I trust you that I don't need this right now," instead of stewing over it. Gradually I was learning to lean fully on God.

"Are you getting out of the house?" Pastor Cliff would ask me.

"No."

"Why not?"

"I feel guilty asking people to watch my kids all the time and don't want to ask unless I really need it."

"Don't you think you have friends who would love to help? You DO really need it!" And he'd urge me to call, or he would pick up the phone and call someone for me.

It's easier for me to suffer in silence—but that is only my pride. And God wanted to do some housecleaning on my pride! Pride, too, is noisy. There were times God would just send people to watch the kids or help around the house when I wasn't expecting it, and there were other times I had to get on the phone and call until I found help—or accept that what I wanted wasn't a "need."

"If you fall, your family goes with you. You have to take care of yourself," Pastor Cliff chided. It's the cardinal rule of care-giving, one many people tend to forget, whether they are parents of small children, taking care of an aging parent, or helping others.

Sometimes a friend would ask me what our lives were like, and then they listened—usually we both ended up laughing or crying. Sitting takes time. Sometimes we said nothing for a few moments, and in that silence, I found comfort because they were with me. There is something incredibly humbling about knowing there's nothing we can do to change a circumstance, something that seems to demand our silence. As if to say, silence is the most we can give, because he is God and we are not. But when we trust him, it is a silence pregnant with God's love.

> *"I will be a Father to you,*
> *and you will be my sons and daughters,"*
> *says the Lord Almighty.*
>
> *~ 2 Corinthians 6:18*

He is the one who promises we are not alone, and keeps his promise. Will we go to him? He calls, beckoning us to sit with him, and enjoy the comfort of silence in his presence. Take time today to nestle your head into the crook of the Shepherd's arm, breathe deeply, and allow him to comfort your soul. ∞

Lean Back

I wish I could promise you that you won't ever sit alone, humanly speaking. We all do at times—and sometimes even when we aren't alone, it feels as though we are.

But I can promise you that God will meet your needs according to his glorious riches in Christ. Have you trusted him to define your needs? Are you willing to set aside pride and ask others for what you need?

I remember walking in the woods that first fall, listening to the leaves crunch under my feet, and God almost audibly urging me, "Seek first the kingdom of God" (Matthew 6:33). Whenever I feel lost and hopeless, I go back to that thought.

Maybe sometimes you have felt that God has failed you. Life will be difficult at times, and there will be things we think are needs that God denies. Give it over to him. Read Matthew 6 every day until you hear him also speaking to you.

> "He calls his own sheep by name and leads them out...He goes on ahead of them, and his sheep follow him because they know his voice. But they will never follow a stranger; in fact, they will run away from him because they do not recognize a stranger's voice."
>
> ~John 10:3-5

You are much more valuable than the sparrows and lilies that speak of God's gentleness and care. Let go of the noise of anger and unforgiveness, of worry and inadequacy, of pride and self. Strain your ear to hear his voice, the voice of one who calls you by name and knows you intimately. Read until you sit in the silence that is pregnant with God's love, read until you hear his voice calling to you. Rest as he comforts your soul. ✺

Chapter Five

GOOD MEDICINE
Injections of Thankfulness

*Learn to laugh at yourself. Then you'll always
have something funny to think about.*

~ *my grandmother*

~ *Day 25* ~

I pray that out of his glorious riches he may strengthen you with power through his Spirit in your inner being, so that Christ may dwell in your hearts through faith.

~ Eph 3:16-17a

The picture of the waterfall in our living room had to come down. Dave had taken it when he taught English in Japan one college summer. How he loved teaching, and how the Japanese people had touched his heart! I can almost hear the white water painting the dozen or more mossy rock-steps with its coolness before turning for one last long splash. The falls carved their intricate path through the wooded hillside and proclaimed, *God's hand has been here, as surely as it has been in Dave's life.*

But the picture was one of the first things to change after we found out Dave had Lyme. The nail it hung on happened to be the only good location to hang his IV bag. We ran the IV every afternoon for about thirty to forty-five minutes.

I felt like a pharmacist as I made up the bags. First I swabbed all of the vials and the bag's injection site with alcohol. I drew up 10 cc's of air and injected it into the bottle of normal saline solution. The vials were tightly sealed, and whatever needed to be removed had to be replaced with something. Injecting the air first enabled the needle's plunger to work like a vacuum, sucking up liquid the glass vial willingly released. I drew up as much saline and injected that into the vial of powdered antibiotic.

I shook it vigorously, making sure every particle dissolved. Then I used a larger needle to inject more air, and withdraw the liquid. The antibiotic vial was always stubborn. At first it would expel readily, but then it made me work harder and harder to get the last of the medicine out. My fingers were sore after several batches. Finally I injected the mixture into the saline solution in the IV bags, and we were ready to go.

Dave had a single lumen central line implanted in the left side of his chest. On the line outside his chest was a luer-lock, a needle-less system for which I was glad. With two small children around, the fewer needles the better. I swabbed both connectors with alcohol, screwed the bag into his line, released both clamps, and hung the bag on the nail to drip. Sometimes Dave would fall asleep during the half-hour it ran. When it was done I replaced the clamps and unscrewed the IV line. Morning and evening we flushed his line with heparin to make sure it didn't clot.

We got used to the waterfall picture being gone, that reminder of the man he used to be. Occasionally visitors would see the IV bag on the nail, and it always brought a chuckle because it was so unlike a hospital hanger. We laughed too.

We were thankful to have a diagnosis at last, and that we could finally begin on the road to treatment, and hopefully healing. It was a relief, in many ways, to begin to let go of some of the anger, to allow hope and thankfulness to come in.

I had been like the inflexible glass vial, unwilling to let go of anger without first being filled—and always God was seeking to fill me, to pour out his love into my heart. After awhile, I didn't want to fight his love any more. It softened me and pushed out my bitterness as God painstakingly worked to withdraw it.

Is there something in your heart today that God is longing to replace with his love?

> And I pray that you, being rooted and established in love, may have power, together with all the saints, to grasp how wide and long and high and deep is the love of Christ, and to know this love that surpasses knowledge—that you may be filled to the measure of all the fullness of God.
>
> ~ Eph 3:17b-19 ⚭

~ *Day 26* ~

A cheerful heart is good medicine,
but a crushed spirit dries up the bones.

~ Proverbs 17:22

Sometimes it's hard for me to keep a heart of thankfulness, but my then four-year-old son Zach showed me how. He used to say, "I need more toys," and I would reply, "We should get rid of some so you can be thankful for what you have."

"I will be thankful!" he quickly replied.

Then one day he asked, "Mom, can we get rid of some of my toys? I have too many." So we went through his room and organized what he could take care of and what was too much.

I said, "Now Zach, I want you to understand that when we give a toy away, it won't be yours any more."

"Will we give them back to my cousins?"

"No, they don't need them. We'll give them to some children who don't have toys."

Then he happily went through his room saying, "Here Mom, you can give this to those other children. My room is bigger now! Thank you, Mommy!"

"And a little child will lead them…"
~Isaiah 11:6

We have so much that Job didn't. We have retained our house. We have our children, and they are such a joy to us, such a comfort. Loving friends and family surround us. All this and more are gifts, blessings from God, not things I have earned.

Job taught us that God is worthy of being worshipped if we have nothing. We don't look to Job's suffering to invalidate our own struggles, but to validate the fact that God is trustworthy— if even Job clung to God, then certainly that's attainable for us.

One week we received a missionary letter, with a picture of a family living in what used to be their home—only two charred walls remained, and no roof. But the owners thanked God for what they had and were organizing a clothing drive to give to those in greater need. The family's loving hearts seared a permanent image in my mind—do we realize what we have?

Another image was etched in my mind from my days working at the International Teams home office—a picture of a small, solitary boy atop a garbage dump that spanned the horizon, looking for things he could sell to make money for his family. There were pictures of homes falling apart, row upon row of tin or cardboard shacks, with no electricity or running water. We take so much for granted.

I wish my grandma were still alive! How I loved to hear her stories about playing in the dirt with my Uncle Roscoe. I wish I could hear again, now that I might have some appreciation, what it was like to lose their farm in the Great Depression. "We had each other!" she would boldly declare. She knew how to have a heart of thankfulness; she earned it through her tears as I am learning to do now. Thankfulness is good medicine.

The battle is in our minds. We can make pain easier—or harder—to bear, depending on what we focus on. This isn't a battle that's won once and for all. It's won in moments, in finding satisfaction in what we do have, what we can do, rather than focusing on what we don't have and can't do. Pride looks to big accomplishments and assigns them great value. And these things do have some value. But humility cheerfully makes the best of limitations and does with them what it can, allowing God's grace to cover the rest.

> The LORD does not look at the things man looks at.
> Man looks at the outward appearance,
> but the LORD looks at the heart.
>
> ~ 1 Samuel 16:7b

~ *Day 27* ~

I know what it is to be in need, and I know what
it is to have plenty. I have learned the secret of
being content in any and every situation, whether
well fed or hungry, whether living in plenty or in
want. I can do everything through him who gives
me strength.

~ Philippians 4:12-13

In Dave's second to last sermon, he talked about the "secret of being content." "Whether well fed or hungry," Paul says, "whether living in plenty or in want." These were the "all things" he could do. He could bear and endure life no matter what it brought, because he knew the secret of being content.

I have only been truly hungry once. I don't mean fasting, or being ready for a meal, but hungry when eating was not in my control. We were leading a teen mission team in rural Tennessee, repairing two houses. The monthly checks that the families depended on were late that month, and neither family had food. One family borrowed food from a neighbor for dinner the previous night. The other had eaten the last of their food that morning. The students joyfully pooled their money and went grocery shopping to surprise the families.

We worked late that night to make up for the time we spent shopping. When we got back to our campsite around seven, we were sweaty, dirty, smelly, and still needing to build a fire and cook dinner. It was eight hours since we had eaten, and I didn't know it yet but I was pregnant. The tantalizing aroma of chili and grilled cheese sandwiches gnawed at my nauseated stomach, but I could tell there wasn't enough food again. All week I had been hungry, but I assumed it was from the work and fresh air, and from the inexperience of the new host-coordinators in knowing how much food to buy for the teams they brought in.

When we finally sat down to dinner, our coordinators had a special surprise for us. They gave us rubber bands to join our wrists to each other for the meal. I was so hungry I couldn't see straight. The painstaking effort of coordinating every movement of my hands with the people on either side of me made me furious, but the message was clear. This is a small picture of what it feels like to have your "hands tied" and not be able to provide for your family the way you want to. This is what it feels like to have to depend on others. This is a glimpse of what it's like to be truly hungry. For us it was only one meal. It was not daily living, but it was enough to give us a new compassion for the families we served.

Dave reminded us in his sermon that we don't have to be complacent and just give up. But we can accept God's answer as Paul did. He learned to be content, day after day, whether well fed or hungry, in prison or free. He was content with what he had in the moment—he even learned to be content despite his "thorn in the flesh." That is the kind of contentment we are struggling to take hold of.

How did Paul accomplish this amazing feat? *Through* Christ. He relied on Christ's presence in him to sustain him, trusted in God's goodness to provide for him, drew on Christ's suffering to encourage him towards perseverance—and fully rested in God's character, intentions, and providence:

> I will make an everlasting covenant with them: I will never stop doing good to them, and I will inspire them to fear me so that they will never turn away from me. I will rejoice in doing them good and will assuredly plant them in this land with all my heart and soul.
>
> —Jeremiah 32:40-41

Do you hear God's passion for his people? Take a few minutes to meditate and enjoy his love for you.

Thankfulness takes practice. If I think about my my husband in terms of what was—the intimacy lost, the conversations, the games, the things we could do, the sharing of the marriage bond—my heart grieves. And not that it shouldn't—but I can't live in the past. I can't live in the land of what-ifs or if-onlys.

Nor can I live in the future. I'd like to believe Dave will be healed before he goes to heaven. I pray and help him in any way I can. But if I only live for the husband I'll have tomorrow, then I don't love and value my husband today, and I deny God has a plan for me now.

I can only live today. I plan for tomorrow, I remember yesterday with fondness mixed with sadness, but I will love Dave today. He is my husband. Though my life isn't easy, I find strength, because my hope, refuge, and sanctuary are in God. My true and final rest is only found in trusting Christ more than myself. He will *never* stop doing good to me. He *rejoices* in doing me good.

When are you living? Does God have to meet your demands in order for you to find contentment? Or are you aware that God has something for you now, today, a precious gift he wants to give you in the midst of your trial?

These are hard words to live; you may not be ready for them now. Many days I'm not. That's okay. God is gracious. He is our Abba-Daddy who gathers us in His arms and holds us close when we hurt.

> He tends his flock like a shepherd:
> he gathers the lambs in his arms
> And carries them close to his heart;
> he gently leads those that have young.
>
> ~ Isaiah 40:11 ❧

~ *Day 28* ~

> For you know that it was not with perishable things such as silver or gold that you were redeemed from the empty way of life handed down to you from your forefathers, but with the precious blood of Christ, a lamb without blemish or defect.
>
> ~ 1 Peter 1:18-19

The joy is not in the trial—the suffering and grief and turmoil.

The joy is in God drawing us close.

But if we don't look for that, we could totally miss God's passionate love for us, making our trial so much worse, harder, lonelier—stealing its fruit and forsaking the joy of close communion with him.

It seems odd, on the surface, that God would use a trial to bring joy. But when the strength of this world is stripped away, he moves us to look for true strength, true riches, true worth— he beckons us to discover his over-abundant love, the glorious God for whom we were made, our only completer, our only fulfillment and joy.

I am not a "have not." I am a have. I have a husband, a man whom God highly values. The most precious thing in all of heaven, the blood of Christ, was given for Dave. The God of the universe, a holy God full of glory, has a plan for each one of us, and right now his plan is for me to care for Dave. It is a holy task. How he values me! I am humbled in spirit that God would esteem me for such a task as taking care of his beloved one.

And God has given me the blessing of two children, to care for and to raise and train and reveal his character and love to. What blessing, what honor is mine.

We live our lives to reveal Christ to the people we know and meet. What a holy, awesome, incredible, humbling role.

If God counts us worthy to give full-time care and attention to one of his children, who are we to argue with God? Why shouldn't we find a way to be satisfied and take joy in that? It's not that we don't try to improve our circumstances, but that we trust God for the outcome.

We can put our full trust in him and *know* he provides for every need. He will not withhold something we need to accomplish his purposes. If we don't have health or money or anything else that seems necessary in this life, God can still be glorified. And we can find comfort.

We have the doting love and attention of the Most High God. We have more riches in Christ than we could ever find time to thank God for. We bow before his kingly throne, and he extends the scepter of his love to us, he beckons us to come, he seeks us and draws us into his embrace. Do you hear him? Do you know his over-abundant grace? Do you listen for him to say your name?

"Be still," he calls, *"and know that I am God"* (Psalm 46:10).

Betsy George, daughter of author Bob George, wrote when her father was dying in the hospital:

> I had my quiet time sitting at the side of Dad's bed, enjoying the early morning tryst for him. As I poured out my weary exhaustion, the Lord met me with a promise: *"I will pour out on the house of David...a spirit of grace and pleas for mercy..."* ~ Zechariah 12:10. And then I began to think of what Dad would say were he cognizant of his surroundings.
>
> "Well, waiting at the hospital is just what we do today." And so it is. With the grace God gives we all will continue to wait and walk with him in this valley of shadows. He doesn't have to explain what he does; he himself is enough.[20]

Lean Back

Dave ended that sermon on the secret to being content with a funny analogy: Imagine riding on a small, 13-seater plane across country. Suddenly, Boom! The engine blows up and the plane is engulfed in flames. The pilot comes over to the door with parachutes and says, "Everyone needs to jump now!"

The first person says, "I have a request. I'd like a pink parachute." The captain explains that he can't grant that request and gently nudges the person out the door.

The next person requests, "Can you guarantee I won't get nauseated on the way and take away my fear of heights?"

"No, I'm sorry, I can't do that, but this parachute will get you there, go."

The third person says, "I know another way, why don't we just ride the plane until it crashes and maybe we will be okay?"

Then another chimes in, "Let's ride a little longer, until we're closer to the ground, and then jump."

"You don't know what you're saying," the captain says. "The parachute will get you there. It is able to do the job."

If we have trusted Christ with our very life, our salvation, our eternal well-being, we can also trust him along the way. Have you heard God's calling on your life to find contentment with what you have—even if it's not what you want? He will never stop doing good to you. Go to him with a thankful heart. He truly is good medicine.

Lord, give us singleness of heart and action, minds that are fully set on you—that we may fear you for our own good and the good of our children after us. Amen.

(Based on Jeremiah 32:39) ❧

Part Two

A GLIMPSE OF HIS GLORY
Character and Hope

Mine to Keep
by Helen Keller

They took away what should have been my eyes
(But I remembered Milton's Paradise)

They took away what should have been my ears
(Beethoven came and wiped away my tears)

They took away what should have been my tongue
(But I had talked to God when I was young)

He would not let them take away my soul—
Possessing that, I still possess the whole.[21]

Chapter Six

WHO IS GOD?
Searching with Heart and Soul

*It was as if God said to him, "Job, I am your an-
swer." Job was not asked to trust a plan but a
Person, a personal God who is sovereign, wise,
and good. It was as if God said to Job: "Learn
who I am. When you know me, you know enough
to handle anything."* [22]

~ R. C. Sproul

~ *Day 29* ~

Where can I go from your Spirit?
Where can I flee from your presence?
If I go up to the heavens, you are there;
if I make my bed in the depths, you are there.
If I rise on the wings of the dawn,
if I settle on the far side of the sea,
even there your hand will guide me,
your right hand will hold me fast.

~ Psalm 139:7-10

Dave had responded so positively to the IV antibiotics at first. There were five wonderful days where he was just like his old self—as if he'd never been gone. But that honeymoon phase quickly faded, and his warmth and personality seemed to slip away into a shell. Weeks rolled into months—November, December, January—what happened?

I felt so confused about Dave, and spiritually lost. If we are to know Christ, what sense does it make to try to know someone who hides himself, who is, in a sense, not here?

*How do we move from knowledge of God
to knowing God?*

Journal

I don't know why God didn't answer Job's questions. It makes me feel rejected by God. I feel like God considers our lives trivial—as if it is easy for him to make happen what is devastating to us. Or "allow to happen," our euphemistic phrase in which we try to say God is both in charge and not to blame.

I always felt Dave was in there somewhere, but where? He came out briefly at times—and then other times didn't understand humor, my touch seemed to hurt, his memory failed him. Who was he now? And who was I? What did it mean to be married to someone who couldn't always respond to me? What in the world was God doing?

Dave—there, but not there. God—there, but not there. Would this be life from now on? Never alone and yet acutely abandoned—life seemed terrifying and unbearable.

I thought God was too far away, my fears of the future overwhelmed me and I wanted to run away—but God didn't ask me to live the future today. Day by day God showed me he is near.

> "I love God because he listened to me, listened as I begged for mercy. He listened so intently as I laid out my case before him. Death stared me in the face, hell was hard on my heels. Up against it, I didn't know which way to turn; then I called out to God for help: "Please, God!" I cried out. "Save my life!" God is gracious—it is he who makes things right, our most compassionate God. God takes the side of the helpless; when I was at the end of my rope, he saved me"
>
> ~Psalm 116:1-6, THE MESSAGE ☙

~ *Day 30* ~

Let him who walks in the dark,
who has no light,
trust in the name of the LORD
and rely on his God.

~ Isaiah 50:10b

Like those first days of treatment, three years later and then eight years later, I again watched hope offer its olive branch briefly and then dissolve into a dream when I reached for the mirage. For a few cherished moments, Dave and I were able to talk deeply; then those times dissolved and his thinking was confused again.

My world went dark.

I retraced the steps in my mind, trying to find where I had lost track of myself and God. Sometimes God, too, seemed to be a mirage.

"God, it's taking so long for Dave to heal!" And then God, somehow mysteriously near again, reminded me that Dave went fifteen years undiagnosed, but never out of God's sight.

At times like this, I'm filled with fears and seem to run frantically, looking desperately for something to hold onto. God beckons me to rest and to feed on his Word. Too exhausted even to rest, I cry out, *"God, please carry me!"*

Like the time when Elijah was running for his life from Jezebel, God wakes us in our fearful delirium and brings us food by his angels.

> Then [Elijah] lay down under the tree and fell asleep. All at once an angel touched him and said, "Get up and eat." He looked around, and there by his head was a cake of bread baked over hot coals, and a jar of water. He ate and drank and then lay down again.
>
> ~ I Kings 19:5-6 ✍

~ *Day 31* ~

> The angel of the LORD came back a second time
> and touched him and said, "Get up and eat, for
> the journey is too much for you." So he got up
> and ate and drank. Strengthened by that food,
> he traveled forty days and forty nights until he
> reached Horeb, the mountain of God.

> ~ I Kings 19:7-8

The journey was too much for Elijah. As it often is for us—
and as it was for Job. Though Job never forsook God, at times
he understandably became blinded by bitterness and lost sight
of who God is. He accused God of "mock[ing] the despair of
the innocent," taking pleasure in oppressing him, and "smil[ing]
on the schemes of the wicked" (Job 9:23, 10:3). He wandered in
this painful desert of misunderstanding God for close to forty
chapters, with friends who only poured salt in his wounds, until
God himself appeared. And we, too, hunger and thirst for the
presence of God to relieve us.

I often found solace in God at Oakdale, the local forest preserve. There in the woods or by the creek I could quiet my
heart, hear God calling to me, and talk with him in the natural
way I had as a child.

Journal

*Oh, what a beautiful fall-like day! I asked God to give me a word
today, and he did. "Seek first the Kingdom of God." Matthew 6 again.
I still seek so much else first.*

*I smelled a campfire; I miss that smell. That's a Dave-and-Merry
smell. I listened to the crunch of gravel under my shoes that Dave
loves, and the crackling of leaves that I have always loved. I watched
and listened to the gurgling creek, so like where I grew up. My parents*

gave me the most wonderful gift, growing up in the beauty and silence of our old farmhouse in the valley.

There I knew the journey was not to run away from what I feared, but to find something to run toward, as Elijah had. To run towards the One who has his heart set on us.

Does he take pleasure in our pain, as Job wondered? No! He is passionate, jealous for our love. When he comes to us, the earth trembles and quakes.

He is so zealous for us, that he covenants with us on pain of death. If he would forsake us, may he be slain, cut in two, as the pieces of the animals he walked between when he covenanted with Abraham.[23] If he would forsake us, may the warrior's bow, aimed at him after every storm, let loose.[24] The rainbow is not merely beautiful and peaceful—it is a sure sign of his promise. He will never leave us before, during, or after our storms. In your trial remember the warrior's bow.

And quite the contrary to Job's question—he experienced pain of death *for* us. He thundered down to rescue us from trial and suffering infinitely more severe than the storm that consumes our minds now and makes us doubt his love. No, he is ever faithful, ever passionate in his love for us, ever seeking us in every way that we might turn and truly take comfort in our union with him. ❧

~ *Day 32* ~

Trust in the LORD with all your heart
and lean not on your own understanding;
in all your ways acknowledge him,
and he will make your paths straight.

~ Proverbs 3:5-6

God brought this message home to me one day when I was traveling on the highway to my Mom's. There was a semi in front of me—and I hate driving behind trucks! I can't see the road in front of me, and I want that control. But I remembered another time behind a semi, a dark night in a swirling, blinding blizzard. How grateful I was for a pair of red lights to follow. I couldn't see the road; the lines were washed out in the storm. But I had that truck to follow. I could rest a bit and trust in those lights to help me see what way to go.

We want to see what's ahead, how long before our loved one gets well, what path we should take, how we will get there—but God doesn't offer us that view. We plead, "Show me the way," and God responds with eyes full of compassion, "You need to see Jesus, because *he is the way.*" We want a plan to trust, but God continues to offer the person of Christ.

Our understanding tries to tell us that God's goodness, love, and mercy are evidenced by the circumstances of our lives. We look at the world and think that God is defined by what we see. But that is taking our eyes off of him. If we are to survive our crises, we have to be firmly convinced of God's goodness and love no matter what is happening in our lives. When we know God, we know enough to handle anything.

So we fix our eyes not on what is seen, but on
what is unseen. For what is seen is temporary,
but what is unseen is eternal.

~ 2 Corinthians 4:18 ଈ

~ *Day 33* ~

Cast your burden upon the LORD
and he will sustain you;
he will never allow the righteous to be shaken.

~Psalm 55:22

He doesn't promise to take away our burden; he promises to sustain us. I find such great comfort in that because it's easy to lapse into self-doubt when it seems God isn't answering our prayers—meaning he isn't making the trial end.

I've tried to teach my children to not only pray for what they want, but to pray for the strength and the endurance, patience and love to walk with the Lord humbly, no matter how God answers and no matter what he brings into our path.

Interestingly, the word "burden" in this verse can also mean, "what he has given you." We don't often talk about burdens as coming from the Lord, or afflictions as being from his hand—though in the Old Testament this is common language. It's the truth Job understood when he said "Blessed be the name of the Lord." And Job 42:11 speaks of Job's relatives comforting him for all the adversities that the Lord had brought him—even though Satan did the actions, the Lord allowed it.

That's hard for us to understand; it brings about painful questions or even attacks on God's character. This concept led to the Lord's confrontation with Job:

> "Brace yourself like a man; I will question you, and you shall answer me. Would you discredit my justice? Would you condemn me to justify yourself?
>
> ~ Job 40:7-8

Would we?

Who is this God who confronts us? Is he compassionate, powerful, caring? Job meets his maker in chapters 38-42:

God brings the morning to expose wickedness—he hasn't abandoned this world; he restrains it from being as wicked as it could be (a sobering, terrifying thought).

He knows not only our battles but stoops to get involved and uses all the forces of nature to do so.

He sends rain to water a desolate wasteland—God even cares about the land where no one lives; he satisfies it.

He feeds: The animals depend on God for food; they cry out to their provider, sustainer. He provides for the strong, powerful hunters: the lioness and lion. And he provides for the weak: the raven's young, wandering for lack of food. We cannot trust the most powerful beast on earth to feed us—God feeds us.

He is midwife to the mountain goat, counting the months until she gives birth. He sees all, he cares. He has not abandoned any part of creation—or us.

God gave no wisdom to the ostrich, but the hawk flies by his wisdom and the eagle soars at his command. He gave the horse its strength, beauty, grace, power, and courage.

Supreme: "Will the one who contends with the Almighty correct him?" We contend, we wrestle...but don't correct.

He is clothed in glory and splendor, honor and majesty.

God created the behemoth, strong, not afraid of man or nature, a creature man is unable to trap—but God is in control of this powerful beast. And he is in control of the powerful forces in our lives, the things we have no hope of capturing or subduing. Our condition is hopeless but for God's strong arm, hopeless but that we trust in his justice, his protection.

He is King. The leviathan is more powerful, more terrifying than the behemoth. A beast that won't beg for mercy or become a pet; a creature that can't be harpooned. Its protection is impenetrable and its weapons make the mighty terrified. It is king over all the proud. And the Lord is king over it.

Nothing can thwart the leviathan—and even more so, nothing can thwart the plans of God.

God cares about our state. Four times in just two verses, he tenderly refers to Job as his servant.[25] The Lord vindicates Job before his friends, and is anxious to declare Job's innocence in saying that he spoke rightly when the friends did not.

At a time in history when man was straying from God and learning to worship creation, it was important for God to remind mankind of the creator. And we still stand in awe today.

God has sustained me and walked with me, carried me and wept with me for all these years. I know he cares and is in control. Psalm 55:22 reminds me, it's in his nature to strengthen us, to be with us. I don't have to be afraid that somehow I've fallen from his good graces if he doesn't answer a prayer as I want.

We tend to think answers should be immediate, healing should be now, promises must be proven. And yet…Sarah was barren for 90 years, and lived the first 65 years without any promise of hope. The man born blind was blind for 30 years. The woman who had an issue of blood bled for twelve years. The heroes in Hebrews 11 did not receive what was promised. Surely they all longed and hoped for something different, and sought the Lord for answers, for help. Waiting was in God's plan for them. Sustaining was in his plan for them.

Daily we learn to rely on him and not this world.

Oaks of righteousness won't be shaken because their roots have dug down deep for water in times of drought. They have found water to survive even in the worst of conditions, years of little growth…but the Water of Life was with them.

But even oaks can die, if they are cut off from the water supply. That daily habit of casting our burden upon the Lord and looking to him for our sustenance is our life. ଈ

~ *Day 34* ~

"Simon, Simon, Satan has asked to sift you as
wheat. But I have prayed for you, Simon, that
your faith may not fail. And when you have
turned back, strengthen your brothers."

~ Luke 22:31-32

We all want to believe in a God who rescues us before
things get too bad. But what about the God who doesn't do
that—who is the God we believe in? Do we believe in the God
who gives Satan permission to "sift us as wheat," as Satan did to
Peter? When we are devastated, is our God still powerful?
When our lives are ruined, is our God worthy of praise?

Our praise is conditional if it is only based on how God's
works bless us. And when they don't, we cling to what he will
do for us—and yes that's true, but we miss what's foundational
about God's character that is worthy of praise as long as we
base it solely on his blessings. Do we love the ruler of the universe if he leaves us in the pit? If we cannot say yes, we don't
understand God and our praise is worthless.

I had been asking so many questions. Where is God? Why
doesn't he help us? Why did he allow this to happen to us? The
common questions we all ask when we hit hard times. These
questions can sometimes lead us into a deeper honesty with
God and ourselves. But I found often that there were no satis-
fying answers, because like Job, we only have a partial view.
Pursuing them had the potential to leave me feeling bitter and
frustrated and utterly alone. They poured salt in my wounds.
They led me to the challenge Job posed to God—is God truly
just? They led me to the "words without knowledge" that
"darken" God's counsel (Job 38:2, NASB).

They are the questions Job asked, but not the one God answered. The one God answered provides an incredible healing

balm that leads me to strength, and that question is "Who is God?"

I began to realize through our suffering that maybe I really didn't know who God is—although I knew only he could help us. I wanted to rely on knowledge, but knowledge could only take me so far.

I needed God's view. The strong tower, the tower that rises above the city and sees the full scope of what's going on. I needed the very presence of God.

> Do not be anxious about anything, but in every-thing, by prayer and petition, with thanksgiving, present your requests to God. And the peace of God, which transcends all understanding, will guard your hearts and your minds in Christ Jesus.
>
> ~ Philippians 4:6-7

I wrestled every day to fight worry with the Word. I meditated on Philippians 4:6-7 often. I made my faith test its bounds. The peace God offers is not simply *from* him—it's an extension of him, it's a God-sized peace, it's his very presence guarding us.

When a lifeguard rescues a drowning swimmer, that swimmer flails in fear until, with strong arms underneath, the rescuer says "Be still. Don't fight." Our Rescuer who passes through the water with us, with strong arms underneath, who sees all and knows all that we can't see and know, beckons us to cling to him, to lay our head down on his shoulder and rest in faith.

Faith that endures says, "I would like to be rescued, but I submit to your will and trust in you." Faith has the character of God firmly in its view and knows God so well that the heart and mind are guarded in Christ Jesus. We can't see all. We can see him. ∽

~ *Day 35* ~

> They came to Philip, who was from Bethsaida in Galilee, with a request. "Sir," they said, "we would like to see Jesus."
>
> ~ John 12:21

What is the object of our faith?

Is faith about the degree to which we believe God will do what we want? Do we have to receive the answer we want, to know we have seen God move in our lives? Are we merely seeking answers…or are we seeking Jesus?

If our faith depends on what God does for us in our circumstances, then we miss part of who God is and our relationship is never secure. There's an underlying level of fear each time God doesn't "come through" for us. We don't know and trust his character. Knowing God is what brings us peace.

Peace is hard on many levels though. When I can't understand why God let's Dave continue to suffer, fear, resentment, and rage leave me too confused to see God. Other times I trust, but have felt it's almost traitorous to say I have a peace about our circumstances when Dave's condition is so obviously not resolved. After thirteen years of disability, there is no indication that Dave will be healed. But my source of peace is not in the answers—it's in God's character. Most of the time I have peace that God is good, loving, trustworthy, in control—that I can rest in him.

> Trust…does not mean hoping for the absence of pain but believing in the purpose of pain. After all, if my almighty God is really almighty and my heavenly Father is really fatherly, then I should trust that he can and will do what is good for me in this sad world.[26]
>
> ~ *Kevin DeYoung* ∞

~ *Day 36* ~

Even though I walk through the valley
of the shadow of death,
I will fear no evil, for you are with me;
your rod and your staff, they comfort me.

~ Psalm 23:4

Rest, or run? The urges are powerful. I am a woman compelled to go, but in my going and doing I am sometimes running from silence and rest. I have known silence pregnant with God's presence. And I have known silence terrifyingly devoid of any sense that God is near. I run from the latter. He lures me to the former but sometimes I am afraid to trust he will be there.

He will.

The feelings might not always be there. We are not seeking feelings. The results we expect to see from our earthly view might not be there either. We are not seeking our own way.

But his rod of authority proclaims, "I will redeem this time." As we learn to trust, his staff of comfort brings us peace in the valley, in the shadows, in the fears and the unknowns. He knows. He will redeem this time. He, his person, is what we seek.

> "This is the truth about all of us. We flee the presence of God, even while we serve him. We speak to him but avoid his eyes lest they penetrate our defenses and we are exposed. But God pursues and overtakes us; He arrests us only to bless us."[27]
>
> ~ Robert Dunn ✇

~ *Day 37* ~

Then the LORD came down in the cloud and stood there with him and proclaimed his name, the LORD. And he passed in front of Moses, proclaiming, "The LORD, the LORD, the compassionate and gracious God, slow to anger, abounding in love and faithfulness...

~ Exodus 34:5-6

If we want to move from perseverance to character, we have to learn who God is. And the journey may be exhausting. After one of Elijah's greatest triumphs, he was gripped with fear of the evil Queen Jezebel. Life suddenly took a turn he didn't expect. He ran over 100 miles from Jezreel to Beersheba, and then a day's journey into the desert where he hoped to die.

And then God led him another 200-250 miles to Mt. Horeb, also known as Mt. Sinai, the mountain of God—to the cave where God hid Moses in the cleft when he passed by in his glory. The journey was forty days—a mere five or six miles per day, well below the stamina of a man who can run 100. Did he wander in confusion and depression and doubt? Did he sleep much of the time, exhausted from fear and all the running?

But somewhere in the middle, he stopped running *away*, and started running *to*. He still had the questions, the fears, the worries, the unknowns—but now he had a new destination.

Who is God? And will we run away...or to him?

Journal

I am compelled by the great images of scripture—of Job standing before God "like a man," of Elijah and Moses on the mountain, waiting for the presence of God to pass by them, for God to reveal himself to them. God called me to my mountain, to stand and take it like a woman, to see who he is.

> The LORD said, 'Go out and stand on the mountain in the presence of the LORD, for the LORD is about to pass by.' Then a great and powerful wind tore the mountains apart and shattered the rocks before the LORD, but the LORD was not in the wind. After the wind there was an earthquake, but the LORD was not in the earthquake. After the earthquake came a fire, but the LORD was not in the fire. And after the fire came a gentle whisper.
>
> ~ I Kings 19:11-12

I stand as the disease-wind tears my life apart and shatters dreams from all directions, but God is not in the wind...or the earthquake...or the fire.

He stands there with us, as he did with Moses. He is in the still, small voice, beckoning us to the cleft of the rock, waiting to reveal his presence to us.

> "How will anyone know that you are pleased with me and with your people unless you go with us?...And the LORD said to Moses, 'I will do the very thing you have asked, because I am pleased with you and I know you by name.'"
>
> ~ Exodus 33:16-17

"I am pleased with you," he says to us.

> "My ears had heard of you but now my eyes have seen you. Therefore I despise myself and repent in dust and ashes."
>
> ~ Job 42:5-6

"I am pleased with you," he continues to say to us. His Holy Spirit seals his favor. A. W. Tozer says that "faith is the gaze of a soul upon a saving God."[28] God is calling us to see Jesus with our soul, to gaze, to look deeply into his eyes—to know him. ❧

Lean Back

Who is God?

Ever-present
Our security and protection
The God who hears
Our guide, our light in the darkness
Our rest
The one who feeds us
The one whose heart is set on us
Passionate, jealous for our love
The target of the warrior's bow—he will never forsake you
Savior and Rescuer who experienced death on our behalf
The Way
Possessor of all knowledge, wisdom, power, and authority
A personal, knowable God
Good, all the time
In control, all the time
Just
A strong tower—both all-seeing and our refuge
The one who guards our hearts and minds
The rescuer who passes through the waters with us, with strong
arms underneath.
Jesus
Trustworthy
Sustainer. Redeemer
Compassionate and gracious, slow to anger, abounding in love
and faithfulness. He stood with Moses and proclaimed his
name (Exodus 34:5). He stands with you. Always.
He is pleased with you
He knows you by name.
Intimate. Your Beloved.

Have you been running for the last 100 miles or so until you collapsed in exhaustion? Maybe, like Elijah, you have wondered if it would be better to die?

Stop. Sleep. Rest in the palm of his hand. Let his angels tend to you; let them feed you from his Word and with his love.

Are you looking at a 200 mile-long journey and saying, *there's just no way I can make it to God?* Give yourself time to make this journey. Elijah walked a mere five or six miles a day. You don't have to run—and some days you might not be able to walk—that's okay. Rest and he will walk with you, and carry you with strong arms underneath, into his presence.

What is your soul gazing on? I've meditated a lot on parts of Psalm 27 because I feel like verse fourteen especially is God's call to us in all of this: "Wait on the Lord. Be strong and take heart and wait on the Lord." Earlier, verse three says, "though an army besiege me, my heart will not fear...I will be confident."

When we can rely on God's character, then we can truly rest in knowing that he is in control of our seemingly-out-of-control circumstances—we are safe "though an army besiege us."

It does not take away the pain of a sacrifice to know God's character. In fact, I think he feels the pain with us, because that's part of being one. I cannot avoid the pain of this because I am one with Dave and I love him. I think the same is true with God and us and how he feels our pain. But knowing God's character brings peace in the turmoil, understanding to the unanswered questions, and a sense of rest that is in God and not in anything humanly describable. Knowing God's character gives us hope in this mysterious and wonderful union we have with him. &

Chapter Seven

FIGHTING THE BATTLES
When it's Time to Change Tactics

What is not possible to us by nature,
let us ask the Lord to supply by the help of his grace.[29]

~ The Rule of St. Benedict

~ Day 38 ~

> "Do not pray for easy lives, pray to be stronger men. Do not pray for tasks equal to your powers, pray for powers equal to your tasks. Then the doing of your work will be no miracle, but YOU shall be the miracle.
>
> ~ Phillips Brooks

That elusive word: healing. How often do we long for that miracle, that touch from God's hand that so assures us he is real, he loves us, hasn't forgotten or rejected us. "Hope deferred makes the heart sick" (Proverbs 13:12).

So how do we live without our deepest longings fulfilled? We give them to God, and pray that he will use them and be glorified through them—whether he changes them, fulfills them, or leaves them as they are: longings unfulfilled.

What can God do with brokenness, with emptiness? Paul said that "when I am weak, then I am strong" (2 Corinthians 12:10), and yet none of us want pain and suffering. Why not? Why, if God gives us strength through our trials and troubles, would we not embrace them, not welcome them as if welcoming the very presence of God? *Come, God, and work through me—do what I alone cannot do.*

We long for the eradication of pain, and not wrongfully so. But perhaps sometimes we are so focused on making that our goal that we miss God's gentle whisper. The whisper Elijah heard on Mt. Horeb when he was filled with fear for his life and a world of hurt, wondering if anyone else was left who loved the Lord. The tender whisper of Christ, our Beloved, beckoning us to lean into his shoulder and rest.

Perhaps you've lived through the storm, the earthquake, the rumblings and terror, and God has been in none of them—but have you waited for the whisper? Listen for him; he delights in being good to us.

Maybe if God is not changing our circumstances, he wants to change us instead. Maybe he is calling us to be a different kind of miracle. ∞

~ *Day 39* ~

> "Remember how the LORD your God led you all the way in the desert these forty years, to humble you and to test you in order to know what was in your heart, whether or not you would keep his commands."
>
> ~ Deuteronomy 8:2

Sometimes it's easy to think if I just learned some lesson or prayed the right way, then God would answer in my favor. Other times there is something about saying that we're going through our trials in order for God to teach us a lesson that rubs me the wrong way—although God does teach me things, and I want to be teachable. *Am I "dumber" than others that I need such a harsh method to learn? Am I so slow-witted that I can't figure out this elusive thing God wants me to learn and so end my pain?*

These thoughts become like "cords of death" and "torrents of destruction" (Psalm 18:4-5) coiled around me in a sea of fear like so many arms of a giant squid, choking out life and strangling my faith. Exhausted I come up, sputtering for air.

What is the purpose of trials? In school, tests are not tools for learning, but assessments of what we've learned. Scripture shows that this is God's intent as well. In 2 Chronicles 32:31 God tested Hezekiah *"to know everything that was in his heart."*

And what does God find in our hearts?

Like Job, I rightly insist the pain is undeserved. And like Job...there is an element of pride in my way, blocking my view of the holy, righteous, all-powerful—and loving Rescuer.

God has not sent pain to drown me. Pride is silenced when we remember that Jesus was made perfect through suffering (Hebrews 2:10). Would we say he is dimwitted? "Less than" us in any way? So, if we also suffer, then we can know God is fulfilling his promise to make us like him (Hebrews 2:10-11).

God didn't abandon Christ, and he has not abandoned us.

Instead, pain tests the bounds of our faith in God. Can he bring good even out of this tragedy, this unfair circumstance, this horror? The world says, no. But God says we are his and he will make us like him. Along the way, he gives us perseverance.

Perseverance is more like a muscle than a lesson. It doesn't grow unless we are tested. When muscles are strengthened, they become hard like rocks. And we will be like the Rock when we have finished the test (hopefully it's not forty years in the desert!). We need to persevere "so that when [we] have done the will of God, [we] will receive what he has promised" (Hebrews 10:36).

Is God trying to teach us something? Is he chastening us? Should we question whether our faith is sufficient? I believe we should humbly be willing for God to say "yes" to any of these.

But it's easy to get tripped up in this process. We may not know until heaven *why* God allowed certain pains in our lives. We don't want stopping the pain and introspection to become the overwhelming focus of our lives. Our heart's cry instead is, "Show me Jesus. I want to see you."

It's so easy to strain for pain-free instead of holding out for the blessing as Jacob did when he wrestled with God. God instead wants us to face the pain when it's inescapable—to walk through it with him. To know in faith that he will bring something good out of something awful. This is not a trite panacea that eradicates grief, but a truth that fully acknowledges our sorrows. This is what he has equipped us to do. Like in childbirth, we can fear and fight and make the pain worse, or we can choose to work with it.

> "Faith is not necessarily the power to make
> things the way we want them to be;
> it is the courage to face things as they are."[30]
>
> ~ *Ronald Dunn* ℘

~ *Day 40* ~

> For no one can lay any foundation other than the
> one already laid, which is Jesus Christ. If any
> man builds on this foundation using gold, silver,
> costly stones, wood, hay or straw, his work will
> be shown for what it is, because the Day will
> bring it to light. It will be revealed with fire, and
> the fire will test the quality of each man's work.
> If what he has built survives, he will receive his
> reward. If it is burned up, he will suffer loss; he
> himself will be saved, but only as one escaping
> through the flames.

~ 1 Corinthians 3:11-15

The questions come, sometimes spoken, sometimes only written on people's faces or hidden in their hearts: *Why has God let this happen? Why doesn't God do something? When will this end?* The unanswerable questions.

But there is a question that Dave taught me before all this happened that is far more important, more pertinent, that I am challenged by and I challenge you with: How will we respond? How do we respond to a God who doesn't rush down and rescue us? How do we respond to our Protector when we don't feel protected?

God does not diminish because he doesn't answer on our terms. Shadrach, Meshach, and Abednego went into the fire knowing their fate was in God's hands and said, "Even if not…" (Daniel 3:18). Even if God would not rescue them they would cling to him. We are in the fire, what will we believe? We each build on the foundation of Christ.

May the wood, hay and stubble be burnt up in the flames, and the precious metals and jewels come forth more beautiful.
ಬಾ

~ *Day 41* ~

I cry aloud to the LORD;
I lift up my voice to the LORD for mercy.
I pour out my complaint before him;
before him I tell my trouble.
When my spirit grows faint within me,
it is you who know my way.
In the path where I walk,
men have hidden a snare for me.

~ Psalm 142:1-3

Who is God? How will we respond? What is the utility of suffering? These questions come together like three strands of a cord that cannot be broken. They interrelate—and suffering becomes either a lens through which we see God more, or a reflection of blinding light that burns and hardens the soul.

I felt at times that suffering was my enemy to wage war against, especially when I was battling our insurance company.

Months of red tape followed. Even doctors couldn't agree what the standard of care should be. How was I supposed to figure it out? But I came out "guns blazing" anyway—to do less than fight with all I had felt like abandoning my husband. My war with Lyme felt like a losing battle; perhaps this new enemy was conquerable.

Fighting can be lonely business. *God, why won't you help us?* we may cry out. At times, even God seems like another enemy.

Sometimes our hearts give way to fear. On another day we can see God and find peace; but then somehow it all falls apart again, truth eludes us, God evades us, confusion and exhaustion rules. Is there no way out, no hope?

Are you feeling weak today? Are there snares hidden all around, tearing at your heart, tripping you up? The Lord knows your way—lay it all out before him. He will give full ear to your cries. He is the God who hears. ⁓

~ *Day 42* ~

"If I pray to escape suffering, then I'm saying
that suffering is my enemy and I must avoid it...
If I pray to endure suffering, I'm saying that
suffering is my master... If suffering is not to be
either my enemy or my master, what is my relationship to suffering? The answer God gave to
Paul is: suffering must become your servant.

In other words, if you pray to escape suffering,
and God doesn't answer, don't pray simply to endure suffering. Pray to enlist your suffering. Make
it work for you, not against you!"[31]

~ Warren W. Wiersbe

There had to be some way to get help for Dave! When insurance wouldn't cover treatment, I applied to a patient assis-
tance program with a pharmaceutical company. Meanwhile I
spent over a hundred hours online researching another appeal
letter, this time with a lengthy attachment of medical journals.

I found myself in the middle of a war between doctors, insurance companies, legislators, lobbyists, patients, and state
medical boards as I tried to pursue treatment for Dave. His
doctor—and many Lyme doctors—felt that chronic Lyme was
best treated with IV antibiotics. Other doctors disagreed, and
thought that IV antibiotics were too stringent. Some even
thought chronic Lyme didn't exist.

Journal

*All I want to do is help my husband! God, can't you make this eas-
ier for us?*

*In Pastor Cliff's sermon today, something significant he said was
that Christ is the answer, not to solve our problems but to deal with
them. To work through them with his strength and power. We want
them solved, but there are always problems. Why don't we want what*

God offers to us? We want the rescuer, the quick fix, someone to come down and solve everything.

Slowly my mind began to shift—I still wanted to find a way to fight or escape our suffering, to make it end. But in my emotional and physical exhaustion, I began to question whether suffering was merely a "prison" to escape. I began to look for something more.

Who is God now that our world has fallen apart? The shocking answer I found over time is: God is still trustworthy, he is my strength, and I can rely on him.

We can do everything we have the energy to do, but in the end we need to trust God for the outcome. He is the one allowing us to go through this. We feel that our "prison," our enemy to war against, is the circumstance.

But freedom from our real prison is not found when we escape our circumstances, but through trusting God. This is because we often discover another prison in our mind, one that is more insidious, more confining, and more damaging.

Pride, fears, doubts, lies…what imprisons you? ❧

~ *Day 43* ~

Look to my right and see; no one is concerned for me.
I have no refuge; no one cares for my life.
I cry to you, O LORD; I say, "You are my refuge,
my portion in the land of the living."
Listen to my cry, for I am in desperate need;
rescue me from those who pursue me,
for they are too strong for me.
Set me free from my prison, that I may praise your name.
Then the righteous will gather about me
because of your goodness to me.

~ Psalm 142:4-7

"Set me free from my prison…" Are our prisons of our own making? Is it really *my* prison, one I have self-imposed? And what does freedom truly look like?

In November of 2000, Patti Tennenoff spoke at a local church. She is one of three missionary wives from New Tribes Missions whose husbands were taken captive by Colombian guerillas in 1993, and at that point they didn't know if the men were dead or alive.

I was struck most not by what she was or said, but by what she wasn't, what I didn't hear.

I went hoping to hear her be strong, because I knew if she was strong, I could be strong. Instead she modeled weakness for me. Weakness with dignity.

She was willing to expose her pain, willing to put pride aside. Not in a "pity me, poor me" kind of way, but just in an honest sort of way—not hiding her pain, not dismissing it, not rationalizing or spiritualizing it away.

Patti trusted God, knowing full well that there was no guarantee she'd learn what she yearned to know: the fate of her husband and the other two men taken captive. (The following year, after nine painful years of not knowing, all leads were exhausted. It was decided the men had been killed.)

Relying on God is not a promise of safety as the world defines safety. Nor a promise of provision as the world defines it. It is a complete letting go of self. It is willingly relinquishing all rights and privileges save our inheritance in Christ, which is also in God's hands. It is a willingness to be vulnerable for God.

Journal

Only God is strong, and it's his strength that gets us through, not our own. Until we have no resources to draw on, it's hard to imagine. Praise God he wants more for us than we imagine.

Patti Tenenoff said that at one point she came to realize that she knew a lot about God but didn't know *God. There it is again; who is God? Are we afraid to know God? Do we set aside the potential for relationship in favor of mere knowledge about him, do we trust that more?*

God might be silent; he might make us wait. His Word is always there to feed our minds with news about him. It's touchable, tangible, reliable, trustworthy—not mysterious or silent—and yet we can pursue knowledge from the Bible without pursuing God himself. We need both. *The Word is* living *and* active.

Sometimes I feel a wall there, and I'm afraid to face it. I don't feel I can bear the pain of God's silence, so I don't pursue him. But that first fall I found God was so vocal, so willing to answer my questions and comfort me through the Bible and in prayer. I began seeking him again, and his Word became alive.

> For the word of God is living and active. Sharper than any double-edged sword, it penetrates even to dividing soul and spirit, joints and marrow; it judges the thoughts and attitudes of the heart.
>
> ~ Hebrews 4:12 ∾

~ *Day 44* ~

I eagerly expect and hope that I will in no way be ashamed, but will have sufficient courage so that now as always Christ will be exalted in my body, whether by life or by death. For to me, to live is Christ and to die is gain.

~ Philippians 1:20-21

Rees Howells (1879-1950), a Welsh master of intercessory prayer, told how easy it was to give 100 pounds when his savings account was full, but giving away his last pound was so hard. Then he realized he had to call on the Treasurer when he was in need instead of relying on himself.

To God it is but a small thing to meet our needs, though he does not treat our hearts lightly—but in the whole scheme it is small. His eyes are on our needs for eternity, of which this life is such a small, small part. He will meet our needs, but will it be what we want? And if not, that is the struggle, the pain, the sacrifice we must be willing to part with. If we want God glorified in our lives—there will be times we need to give the last pound.

When Dave is hurting, I want to fall apart. With his pain comes such agony because usually it is not alone. It brings companions in fears about things undone, feelings of worthlessness, depression, tears over the kids he can't be with, the people he can't help or reach, his children and wife he longs to grow with and love. And we wonder, *can God be glorified in a life such as this?*

Sometimes people think I am strong and wonder if they could be this strong if they were going through this, but I am not strong. God is strong. I am weak. I fear, I hate, I get angry, I yell at God, I relinquish, and repent. I am not stone; I am flesh.

Do not think I am strong. God is strong, and I am only following him, asking him for the courage and strength and help to yield at every point he is asking me to yield my life, to submit, to lay my life down in ways I never thought I would need to.

Charles Finney (1792-1875) said that revival is "a new beginning of obedience to God." When I counted the cost (back in college when I rededicated my life to Christ) it was more like a gamble—my rotten, misguided life for God's way in mine, how could that not be worth any risk involved?

It is worth the risk. God can be glorified in our lives. He has not asked anything of me that has not been worth the changes, the inheritance, the joining of his family. But he has asked much, and paying the price has been much different than counting the cost. But I took the gamble willingly, and now he has come for what I promised: me—all of me, in whatever way he chooses to take me. Even to the last pound—or something even more precious to me. ✍

~ *Day 45* ~

How priceless is your unfailing love!
Both high and low among men
find refuge in the shadow of your wings.

~ Psalm 36:7

Journal

My faith has boiled down to three things: God is good, God is loving, and God is sovereign. Do we understand the fear of the Lord? Because I think fear and sovereignty are intertwined. It is a fearful, frightening thing indeed to be in the hands of an almighty God, to realize that everything good in my life is a blessing and not a guarantee. Yet his sovereignty that can terrorize my life is what also holds my eternal security.

Comfort becomes a hope, not a promise. Security is a hope, safety is a hope, sanity is a hope, life on earth is a hope. They are not faith. Faith is being sure of what we hope for and certain of what we do not see. I am not certain I will have any of these things on earth. I am certain that God is good, God is sovereign, and God loves me.

Years ago I made a discipleship commitment to follow God's way. Now I will follow him. The difference may seem subtle to some and painfully obvious to others. No matter, I still must choose to do this. Let God be seen, for he is the only one strong, great, able. I bear up because I pour out to him. He pours me out like a drink offering and when there is nothing left of me I cry out to him and he fills me again. It is a very strange process, and I'm not sure I understand the point at all, except that he is the point. I have nothing and even what I think I have I do not, there is nothing in me or in this world to rely on at all, nothing to count on or trust in, only him. It is a fearful—and wonderful thing to be in the hands of an almighty God.

Thirteen years later, I find these same thoughts are true. The fears are as real and still arrest me from my feelings of security.

But I come back sooner to the reality that walks side by side with these fears; I am safe in the shadow of his wings. When I fall, he swoops beneath me like an eagle does for her young dropping from perilous height—and raises me up on his wings, safe again.

If your suffering is not ending, it may not be your enemy. God may have other plans for you. It may not be something to simply endure and live out your life with. No, strange as it may seem, it may be that suffering is to be your servant. Perhaps God's ultimate purpose may be to use suffering, for a time, to draw you close to the One who suffered for you.

> The Christ we profess to follow was made "perfect through suffering." (Hebrews 2:10). We prefer to be made perfect through success. But grace will not do for us what it did not do for Christ—exempt us from suffering.[32]
>
> ~ Ronald Dunn

Lean Back

> O people of Zion, who live in Jerusalem, you will weep no more. How gracious he will be when you cry for help! As soon as he hears, he will answer you. Although the Lord gives you the bread of adversity and the water of affliction, your teachers will be hidden no more; with your own eyes you will see them. Whether you turn to the right or to the left, your ears will hear a voice behind you, saying, "This is the way; walk in it."
>
> ~ Isaiah 30:19-21

Why do we suffer? Job didn't know and admitted in the end that he spoke with "words without knowledge." Job's friends not only didn't know, but spoke falsely of Job and incurred God's judgment. We may never know in this life, but...

What If?

What if God wants to use my trial as an encouragement to someone? Maybe my faith in the midst of pain will help someone else be faithful.

What if my trial is a reminder of hell? A tiny, dim picture of the horror to come, and a glorious reminder of what he redeems us from? Would we truly understand hell if we didn't experience a microcosm of it on earth?

What if God wanted to use pain to show us how much Christ loves us—the depth he was willing to go to on our behalf? We may be unwilling to go through pain—our Beloved chose it because he wanted us that badly.

What if suffering is God's tool to rescue us from complacency, to drive us to seek Him?

What if God wanted to give us an incomprehensible gift by allowing us to suffer? One we will never fully understand in this life? 2 Corinthians 4:17 says that our trials are light and momentary compared with eternal glory.

We can be open to how God might use suffering in our lives, even if we never get to know why. Can you trust God without knowing why?

If you are leaning back off that precipice, facing an impossible situation and wondering what to do— God's Spirit will uphold you. Drink in deep breaths of his Word—but not just for knowledge; let him speak to you. Cry out to God. Ask him to pray for you when you have no words left to pray. To swoop down under you with strong eagle's wings, and rescue your soul. Don't close your heart to him. He is able—and willing—to bring you through this time.

Life can bring us so much pain. Jesus chose to endure incredible pain, abuse, insults—because you were worth it to him. All that we go through and more, he chose to endure on our behalf. One of the strange ways that suffering is our servant is that it allows us to draw near to him as we marvel at what he chose to go through to rescue our souls. As much as we hurt— he loves us even more. ∽

Chapter Eight

SNAKES IN MY VEINS!
"Though He Slay Me..."

...the greatest suffering I had in the concentration camp was to be stripped of all my clothing and to have to stand naked. I told my sister, "I cannot bear this. This is worse than all other cruelties we have had to endure." Suddenly it was as if I saw Jesus on the cross, and I remembered that it says in the Bible, "They took his garments." Jesus hung there naked. By my own suffering, I understood a fraction of Jesus' suffering. And that gave me strength. Now I could bear my own suffering.[33]

~ *Corrie ten Boom*

~ *Day 46* ~

"It feels like there are snakes in my veins," Dave said. "All over, from my toes all the way up to my head, trying to get out." I wondered how a rational person could hold onto his sanity with such a sensation, and yet he was completely lucid as he told me this.

I shared this quote with Dave:

> I think it is a very common error among the well to think that "with a little more self control" the sick might, if they choose, "dismiss painful thoughts" which "aggravate their disease." Believe me, almost *any* sick person, who behaves decently well, exercises more self-control every moment of his day than you will ever know until you are sick yourself. Almost every step that crosses his room is painful to him; almost every thought that crosses his brain is painful to him; and if he can speak without being savage, and look without being unpleasant, he is exercising self-control.[34]

> ~ Florence Nightingale

Dave always wants to do more, give more, be more. The limitations of illness are infuriating and aggravating, but he seldom shows it. He inspires me every day, but doesn't understand how that's possible.

Illness brings doubts, questions, fears, and Satan sends them as snakes into the veins of our faith. As in a fractured boulder, he slithers through the cracks and threatens the whole structure. You have nothing to give. *Sssssss.* God doesn't care. *Sssssss.* God has abandoned you. *Sssssss.* You're *worthlessssssssss.* The devil is a liar and the father of lies.

What lies about God and your value to him have you wrestled with? And what lies can you renounce? Take some time to capture them today, chart or journal them, or revisit the "Truth and Lies Chart" in Appendix A. Ask God to reveal the truth to you. His covenant with you is eternal—nothing can change his love for you.

> "Can a mother forget the baby at her breast and have no compassion on the child she has borne? Though she may forget, I will not forget you!"
>
> ~ Isaiah 49:15 ∾

~ *Day 47* ~

He was despised and rejected by men, a man
of sorrows, and familiar with suffering. Like
one from whom men hide their faces he was
despised, and we esteemed him not. Surely he
took up our infirmities and carried our sorrows,
yet we considered him stricken by God, smitten
by him, and afflicted. But he was pierced for our
transgressions, he was crushed for our iniquities;
the punishment that brought us peace was upon
him, and by his wounds we are healed.

~ Isaiah 53:3-5

The thought of snakes in Dave's veins gave me chills. But Dave's suffering has not been in vain. It has given me a glimpse into Christ's suffering and his glory. I begin to see the true value of his grace, the depth, length, width, and height of his love.

When God turned my mind from asking *"why?"* to asking *"who?"* I began to see that *"why?"* was really two questions: *"What is the cause of suffering?"* and, *"Can God bring good out of suffering?"*

The question *"why?"* makes suffering into some big riddle to solve—an endless search for a hidden purpose that leaves me isolated and doubting God.

But the cause we can understand—almost. There is suffering because our world is broken by sin. We suffer because of our own sin, because of sins committed against us, because of persecution as a Christian, and because we live in a sinful, fallen world. Dave has Lyme because a disease-ridden tick bit him. My Dad died of kidney failure. My Grandma died of heart failure. I lost a job once due to economic cutbacks. Sin's ultimate end is pain, death and separation from God. That is the basic cause of suffering.

Could God stop it? Yes. Why doesn't he always do that (or at least when it matters most to me or my loved ones)? People have plumbed the depth of that question for centuries. On a broad, general level I think we would never understand the reality of sin and its effect on our lives and relationship with God if God always intervened. It is desperately important for us to understand this most basic principal—sin separates us from God, and eternity is hanging in the balance.

We don't like to think about sin or judgment or being wrong. One of Satan's slithery lies is to get us to think it's not really that bad. But when we don't know how bad sin is, we can't even begin to fathom how much Christ loves us. The Gospel seems impotent.

I also wonder if we could truly love God or have compassion on others if we did not endure the crucible.

But on a personal level I can't see clearly enough to reason it out. Here again I have to rest in God's sovereignty. And I would despair, if it wasn't for the second question.

Can God bring good out of suffering? Yes—and this is where God can bring meaning to what otherwise would be meaningless. We have assurance from God's Word that "in all things God works for the good of those who love him, of those who have been called according to his purpose" (Romans 8:28).

The scripture doesn't say that all things are good, or that evil is good—but that *in* all things God is working for the good of those who love him.

How can I get in step with God's design? Something good can happen? I want to be a part of that! What can I do, what role can I play, in order for God to be glorified? And the answer goes back to that key in my pocket, to Romans 12:1-2, to submitting to God and being a willing, living sacrifice. ❧

~ *Day 48* ~

> When Jesus saw her weeping, and the Jews who
> had come along with her also weeping, he was
> deeply moved in spirit and troubled.
> "Where have you laid him?" he asked.
> "Come and see, Lord," they replied.
> Jesus wept.
>
> ~ John 11:33-35

When Lazarus died, Jesus wept, felt deeply the pain that Mary and Martha felt. It didn't matter that Jesus knew he could bring Lazarus back to life. Understanding didn't erase the pain of the moment. He called out to God and God heard and answered, and Lazarus was brought back to life. And isn't that what we all long for, the God who answers with his power and love? Then we know our prayers have been heard.

Sometimes we get the idea in our minds that if God is sovereign and allows bad things to happen to us that he doesn't care or love us. But the truth is that just like with Lazarus, he weeps for and with us and is greatly grieved over the troubles that happen in our lives. Jesus had the power to keep Lazarus from dying, but he didn't. Jesus had the power to restore life to him, but first he cried. Why did he cry? For all practical purposes Lazarus wasn't really dead because Jesus was in the position of power! And yet, Jesus didn't simply waltz into town, make everything better, and think that that erased all the pain. He lived through the pain with them. He is not only fully God; he is fully man, and fully identifies with us.

We do not have a benign paternal God who looks down from on high with occasional sympathy. We have Emmanuel: God with us. The God whose Holy Spirit has chosen to dwell *in* us. Do we stop and think what this means?

The God who lived through intense anguish on earth continues to choose to live it along with us. He doesn't merely see our pain; he says that "whatever you did for one of the least of these brothers of mine, you did for me" (Matthew 25:40). He is hungry, thirsty, a stranger, naked, sick, and in prison along with us. *With you.*

Like a knight in shining armor, he identifies with our pain as his own and rushes in to defend us. "Saul, Saul, why do you persecute me?" he confronts in Acts 9:4. We are part of his body, bride and bridegroom, vine and branches, intimately connected—and our pain is his pain.

When he says, "never will I leave you, never will I forsake you" (Hebrews 13:5), he means to impart a depth of love that if we truly understood it, would take our breath away.

What you and I live through, often involuntarily, God has chosen to live through with us, intimately, daily, weeping with us. Power doesn't erase pain. Love heals pain.

Here again we meet God's love and God's sovereignty—how will we respond? It is one thing to have everything taken from us, and another thing to offer it to God, saying, "Here is my life, do with me as you will. And if you are willing for me to suffer and you are not going to change things right now, then I am still willing to be your child, and I offer myself to you." A *living* sacrifice.

God knows what He's asking of us. The fact that it's for a good cause does not erase the pain. The pain must be fully known by both God and us in order for there to be a sacrifice at all.

The ironic part is that when we are willing to submit fully to whatever God's will holds for us, we gain strength. We gain courage and peace because our souls are not at war with an oppressor, but children at rest in their Father's arms. &

~ *Day 49* ~

> I want to know Christ and the power of his resurrection and the fellowship of sharing in his sufferings, becoming like him in his death, and so somehow to attain to the resurrection from the dead.
>
> ~ Philippians 3:10

God has given us one of the greatest of all gifts through suffering. It is the gift I would never want but the one everyone has to face, some to a greater degree, some to a lesser degree, all of it real and difficult to us.

To share in his joy, to know Christ fully, we must live as he lived, experiencing both his power and his suffering.

The first part sounds so good until we realize that to understand resurrection we have to understand death and suffering. I don't think I signed up to be that kind of Christian. I thought the Christian life was about comfort, about being relieved of my burdens and fears. It is in part, and that's a much more pleasant side of the message. But if we really want to know and love Christ, then we must be willing to suffer with and for him. It is not enough to remember, recount, and become fully aware of his suffering for us.

We must enter into his suffering
if we are to share in his joy.

I never used to stop and think what it means to become like Christ in his death. I rarely engaged myself in the price he paid. How different from *his* engagement in our pain.

It's easy to see ourselves as victims instead of realizing God has given us a great dignity through our pain. We have the honor to answer, at least in part, Satan's accusation:

> Is God worthy to be loved and obeyed even if He does not bless us materially and protect us from pain?...Is it possible for us to serve God and our fellow humans from a heart of love, regardless of what we may 'get out of it'? Satan would reply, "Absolutely not! True virtue is not possible because God is not worthy and man is not able.[35]
>
> ~ Warren Wiersbe

Satan's accusation must still be answered today, both for ourselves and for the entire heavenly host. Is man's faith futile and even evil, based solely on receiving blessing and thus God's plan is also futile and has failed? Or is man's faith genuine and sincere, resulting in praise and glory for God?

And isn't that the ultimate question? Isn't that why tribulations must come? When they do, will we be ready? Will our faith be strong? Or is it weak, demanding God do what we want?

People right now today, in many parts of the world, are persecuted for their faith. We feel badly but we are more protected. What will we do if the protection is removed?

A strong faith isn't the one that always gets a "yes" answer from God. A strong faith is the one that accepts his answer and praises God. &

~ *Day 50* ~

"These [trials] have come so that your faith—of greater worth than gold, which perishes even though refined by fire-may be proved genuine and may result in praise, glory and honor when Jesus Christ is revealed."

~ 1 Peter 1:7

We are faced with a unique opportunity: the ability to prove on some level that our love is not based on what God gives us, but is because he is worthy of our love.

We have an incredible hope in the thought that our trials can result in praise, glory, and honor. We have a measure of comfort in having something in common with Christ. There is a beautiful, intimate fellowship that is shared in the unity of suffering.

In suffering, we see his face.

Would we look into the eyes of the one who suffered for us and say, your love is not enough for me?

No! May it never be! May we instead begin to comprehend the riches of his tenderness and love and passion for us. May we instead make peace with God's sovereignty.

Through our steadfast faith and love for God we have a great, honor bestowed upon us, to play a role in Christ being glorified. Do we understand that God is worthy of our suffering and our worship? Do we stop to ponder God's incredible value and worth?

God, what do I treasure above you? What have I not left to follow you? Help me draw near, show me what holds me back.

God, I treasure that you have given me an access to you I didn't know before, a depth in you I didn't have, an awareness of your overabundant love I never knew. Thank you for a relationship with you that is beautiful and lasting. Amen. ℘

~ *Day 51* ~

"Now if we are children, then we are heirs—heirs of God and co-heirs with Christ, if indeed we share in his sufferings in order that we may also share in his glory."

~ Romans 8:17

Satan offers us snakes in our veins. God offers us an inheritance, indeed is even willing for us to share in the glory of Christ. Unfathomable!

We are children, heirs—and there is a beauty to be found in sharing in his sufferings. They enable us to share in his glory. Can we even comprehend that God would share such riches with us?

"...He has given us his very great and precious promises, so that through them you may participate in the divine nature and escape the corruption in the world caused by evil desires."

~2 Peter 1:4

We have his great and precious promises. We *participate in the divine nature!* Such wondrous riches, such unity with God, is worthy of our meditation.

My suffering is not a picture of whether or not God loves me, for certainly he loves us dearly. Rather it is an indication of his sovereignty and a great opportunity—will I lay down my life to the extent God calls me to, or go kicking and screaming? ∞

~ *Day 52* ~

For it has been granted to you on behalf of Christ
not only to believe on him, but also to suffer for
him...

~ Philippians 1:29

Perhaps in this world, love will always require suffering. To love Christ requires sharing in his suffering.

Peter turned away at first and denied Christ because he couldn't. He feared that disqualified him from service. Jesus gently restored him though. Do I share in Christ's suffering?

I am not a martyr, but my response can add meaning to my suffering—what do I bear witness to? If by my suffering people only see that I have a hard life, I have not borne witness to Christ. If I play up the martyr-role and use mock-humility, I have not borne witness to Christ. Instead, I have borne witness to myself, and my goal is self-glorification rather than glorifying God.

But if people see in the sufferer's life a steadfast faith, a joy beyond human explanation, a peace that can only come from God, if they see a real and true love for God that is not fake, not a mask, then suffering is transformed into a witness for Christ. When any of us choose to yield ourselves to whatever God has in store for our lives, we suffer for the sake of Christ.

If in humility we don't consider life in our present body worth squelching the hope we have in Christ, the treasure he pours into our jars of clay, the Spirit he fills us with, then we bear witness to Christ. For only Jesus can transform us. Only Jesus can make us capable of saying, and truly meaning, "I consider that our present sufferings are not worth comparing with the glory that will be revealed in us" (Romans 8:18). Only Jesus can make us capable of saying our troubles are "light and momentary" in comparison with the hope we have in him. ❧

~ *Day 53* ~

"Though he slay me, yet will I hope in him..."

~ Job 13:15

What is your hope? Are our trials merely a meaningless happenstance of life, or something God turns into great good?

Suffering is our tool, to pursue him more fully and love him more deeply. It contains hidden treasure—but unearthing the treasure is work.

In our humanity we could turn our backs on God for allowing such pain in our lives. Instead he calls us to yield, to lay down our lives and desires, to be willing for him to live and work in us despite our circumstances. God calls us to trust when circumstances say he isn't who we thought he was, because in reality he is more loving than we've ever imagined. Are we willing to give up self, to lay down our lives for him, to find out who he really is?

"Though he slay me..." Job says. And what is a living sacrifice for, as Romans 12 describes, if not to be slain? That's what one does with a sacrifice, and yet...we are to hope in him. His love sustains us.

Jesus richly pours out his love for us through blood and tears, and he continues to seek us. God's Spirit "intercedes for us with groans that words cannot express" (Romans 8:26b), and the Father sent them both to bring us home. These are some of the hopes and realities we cling to as we lay down our lives.

Though he slays you, hope in him. Seek him. Christ will not disappoint you, but will give you great and wonderful things you never sought. He will give you *himself* and whether we know it or not, that is truly what we want and what we need. ✎

~ *Day 54* ~

But the man who looks intently into the perfect
law that gives freedom, and continues to do this,
not forgetting what he has heard, but doing it—
he will be blessed in what he does.

~ James 1:25

I used to ask, if trials bring perseverance (as James 1 & Romans 5 say), what do I need perseverance for, harder trials? (If that were the case, God could have perseverance!) No, we need perseverance to love God, to love one another, and for our love to become like God's as much as possible: patient, enduring, willing to bear with one another. Do we seek to be that way? Do we ask, "how can I love, what can God do in and through me?" Do we stare intently into the "perfect law that gives freedom" and let the law of love guide how we see ourselves, God, and others?

It is a strange irony that suffering moves us to love and reach out to others. God has greatly gifted us by having people in need among us, and many beautiful saints suffer on our behalf so that we can strip off our crusty hearts and be moved to tears and action.

In suffering we have the gift of loving God with as close to *agape*-love as we can come. Agape is a Greek word that means loving without expecting anything in return. God never stops loving us, but when the blessings of life are removed or hidden, and yet we love him, that is the closest we can get to agape-loving God. The opportunity to give such love is a rare jewel, an expensive gift to treasure in our hearts. He gives us dignity by allowing us to give what is taken. It is the opportunity to be not a victim of life's circumstances, but a friend to God when we yield to him, when we say, "Be glorified, I am yours, and all that have is yours." ☙

Lean Back

I never felt the freedom, despite all that God had given me, to be thankful for Lyme disease itself. That seemed like betraying Dave. Yet after three years, Dave was able to say that he was thankful for the Lyme because God was changing him and drawing him near. God was at long last answering my prayer for God to use this for good in Dave's life.

Years later our son said that God had made him a more compassionate person through his dad's illness. Dave said, "If that's true, then it's worth it."

Have you looked for God to change you? Have you thought about your trial as the most incredible opportunity ever to love God? We are inextricably intertwined with Jesus' suffering—and through it we have an incredible view of God's never-failing love for us. So I say again, though he slays you—hope in him.
ॐ

Chapter Nine

IN A MIRROR DIMLY...
Breaking Pride's Image

I know God will not give me anything I can't handle, I just wish he didn't trust me so much.[36]

~ *Mother Teresa*

~ *Day 55* ~

God opposes the proud
but gives grace to the humble.

~ James 4:6b

"If you don't like our decision, you can get a lawyer and sue us," came the cool reply from the agent at the headquarters of our insurance company. "There is no further appeal process." After many appeals and over 100 hours of research on my part, the insurance company had finally agreed to pay for eight weeks of IV treatment, but Dave's doctor said he needed more than that.

All that fighting, and then...emptiness. I felt I had failed Dave and that God was rejecting me. But there was something else.

As I fought to win the insurance battle, I was also fighting a personal battle on every front. I had to write the perfect appeal, and be the perfect mom, the perfect wife, the perfect caregiver—all with a bottomless tank of patience.

The more I tried to be perfect, the more I failed. I picked at my weaknesses like old scabs, continually open and bleeding because I wouldn't leave them alone. I began to buckle under my sense of obligation to work in as many children's ministry areas as I could—nursery, children's church, AWANA— because I knew how hard it was to find volunteers, and now, with Dave gone, there was no pastor to do that. Slowly I was burning out.

I thought that our trial was more than I could bear, and it was. But so was the burden of self-reliance, the weight of perfectionism, rooted in ugly pride. It is a core issue that must be dealt with if we are going to see God.

Pride is blindness to our need for God. It relies on self for direction, and that's a lonely faith. God wants us to commune with him. Galatians 5:16 says, "Live by the Spirit, and you will not gratify the desires of the flesh." I thought I could use rules to obtain perfection, but it was lifeless. And at every turn I met grace, unmerited favor, instead.

> [Grace] teaches us to say 'No' to ungodliness and worldly passions, and to live self-controlled, upright and godly lives in this present age.
>
> ~ Titus 2:12

The law only shows us the character of God and our need for a savior. It is lifeless, and powerless to change us.

God does not ask us to change ourselves, but to "fix our eyes" upon him. To relinquish ourselves to him. His grace changes us. His beauty, glory, holiness, and love change us. He calls us to daily take our pride to the foot of the cross, and meet grace face to face. ∞

~ *Day 56* ~

I pray also that the eyes of your heart may be
enlightened in order that you may know the hope
to which he has called you...

~ Ephesians 1:18a

Gordon Macdonald, in his book *Ordering Your Private World,* talks about the difference between being driven and being called.[37] The former is meeting needs on our own, while the latter comes from the position of strength—the position that God has already met my needs and that my actions are a result of God's calling instead of a desperate attempt to meet my own needs.

When I am feeling driven, I often struggle with a false belief that God will love me more if I do more for him. This image is of a God who is never really satisfied with me because there's always more I could do, thus more I should do. He is not happy with good or better. He is only happy with best. And I can never achieve best. I falsely believe he can never be satisfied with me, and I can never be what he wants.

But all of this thinking is conformity to the world, and we must leave it, and be transformed. When we are driven, time and accomplishments become all important instead of our relationship with God. Then we stray from God's Word and from prayer, and our thinking gets warped.

Instead, God calls us to an incredible hope, to bring delight to him just by being, and to take joy in our relationship with him.

The LORD your God is with you,
he is mighty to save.
He will take great delight in you,
he will quiet you with his love,
he will rejoice over you with singing.

~ Zephaniah 3:17

~ *Day 57* ~

> We were under great pressure, far beyond our
> ability to endure, so that we despaired even of
> life. Indeed, in our hearts we felt the sentence of
> death. But this happened that we might not rely
> on ourselves but on God, who raises the dead.
>
> ~ 2 Corinthians 1:8b-9

"God won't give you more than you can bear," is a popular Christian sentiment, meant to encourage the person who is suffering or experiencing some trial. Yet when your world is falling apart, it does not encourage; it brings uncertainties and a sense of failure—after all, if we can't handle what we're facing, what does that say about our faith and our God?

To me this thought both denies reality and waters down God's power in our lives. It encourages us to be stronger on our own, and to believe there is something wrong with our faith or we could handle our pains better.

The reality is, there are often things in this life that are so awful, terrible, complicated, overwhelming, or painful that they are, indeed, beyond what we can endure. Paul, famous for his joy in the midst of suffering, the man who sang in prison after being beaten, admitted the hardships of he and his companions were *far beyond* their ability to endure, and despaired. Sometimes we will too.

We can stop striving to be spiritual giants who can bear anything "with God's help." Help is for the hard times only, for getting past that rough spot until we can do it on our own again. We were not made to handle things on our own. Relying on God doesn't ever end. It's a continual, daily process of relinquishing self to God. It's continual communion with him. &

~ *Day 58* ~

In bringing many sons to glory, it was fitting that
God, for whom and through whom everything
exists, should make the author of their salvation
perfect through suffering.

~ Hebrews 2:10

The Greek word for perfection means complete—thus
when God says we are made perfect in Christ, we are "complete," we lack nothing. It's incredible to think of God as the
One who makes us perfect, instead of trying to perfect ourselves.

How was our "Completer" made perfect through suffering?
It is precisely *because* he suffered that we know he can relate to
us and understand us. His suffering motivates us to come to
him and follow him, because he became one of us and yet went
through more than most of us can imagine. He knows what it is
to be given more than you can bear—and yet stand up under it.
His suffering proved his allegiance to God.

Hebrews 5:8 says he "learned obedience through what he
suffered." We know Jesus was never disobedient. But he
learned the full extent of obedience first hand by what he did.
He didn't just have head knowledge; he lived it. His humanity
was made complete because he suffered and yet obeyed God.

Interestingly, the one place where we are commanded to be
perfect is in Matthew 5:48, where we are told to be perfect in
love, as our Heavenly Father is perfect. What a beautiful concept. To be perfect in love has no focus on me, on what I look
like or how I appear. That kind of perfection is very different
than self-righteousness or pride in wanting to hide mistakes.
Pride and love are opposite motivations. Pride protects self;
love protects others. Consider the "model" of perfection:

"Son of man, take up a lament concerning the king of Tyre and say to him: 'This is what the Sovereign LORD says: "'You were the model of perfection, full of wisdom and perfect in beauty. You were in Eden, the garden of God...Your heart became proud on account of your beauty, and you corrupted your wisdom because of your splendor. So I threw you to the earth; I made a spectacle of you before kings'"

~ Ezekiel 28:12-13a, 17

Would we pridefully trust in ourselves for what God has actually bestowed upon us? We can try to become like the model of perfection, but the cost, the downfall is great. Or we can allow Christ to complete us, even through suffering, and seek to be perfect in love—even as he is perfect. ◌

~ *Day 59* ~

The former regulation is set aside because it was weak and useless (for the law made nothing perfect), and a better hope is introduced, by which we draw near to God.

~ Hebrews 7:18-19

There is a better hope introduced by which we draw near to God. Why do we resist that? Why do we look for the old way still?

When people suffer long enough, sooner or later they are likely to wonder, *"Why isn't my sacrifice good enough? I'm giving the best I can give. Why would God allow this to happen to me?"*

But the truth is we have Christ's sacrifice on our behalf—this isn't about being a "good enough person" so that bad things won't happen to us. Christ suffered on our behalf, HE is our sacrifice! There is none better! We can draw near to God.

We may not start out on the path of self-righteousness, but it's hard not to ask why, hard not to think that our suffering isn't fair—hard not to count former good deeds as reasons why we don't deserve to suffer (and maybe someone else does). And before we realize it, God has unearthed a pride we didn't realize was there.

Can we be both perfect & loving? I don't think so. Perfection breeds pride rather than humility.

Who does *perfection* benefit? Self, not others. Perfect people tend to make others feel inferior, inadequate, and discouraged.

Who does *loving* benefit? Everyone around us, and it pleases God. When we sin, God has provided for us. When we learn to love, we may learn to sin less, because the more we love, the less we desire the enticements of this world. Being perfect does not draw people to us or to God. Being loving does. ❧

~ *Day 60* ~

> How great is the love the Father has lavished on us, that we should be called children of God! And that is what we are! The reason the world does not know us is that it did not know him. Dear friends, now we are children of God, and what we will be has not yet been made known. But we know that when he appears we shall be like him, for we shall see him as he is. Everyone who has this hope in him purifies himself, just as he is pure.
>
> ~ I John 3:1-3

When I first accepted Christ, I thought that I might some day in this life quit sinning and move beyond needing Christ's continual forgiveness. I didn't realize the basic truth that the law had no power to make me righteous, and that God had already made me holy and was in the process of making me holy.

My righteous acts are not what make me righteous—they are my loving response to God. Our hope in Christ purifies us—and "when he appears we shall be like him…and *see him as he is.*"

What an incredible hope! I wasted so much of my life trying not to disappoint God by failing and sinning again, that I missed the abundant life he was wanting to pour into me. I wandered in the desert of futility instead of crossing over into the Promised Land where I could "take hold of that for which Christ Jesus took hold of me" (Philippians 3:12). The relationship. We don't outgrow Jesus—we grow *in* him!

Is the cross a source of increasing joy for you, or has it become bland, boring, leaving you with wanting something more?

Do you want to see God?

For so long I was willing merely to survive on the bland diet of manna, provided by God—never realizing the rich foods I could feed on in the Promised Land. I didn't see Jesus—instead of continuing to joyfully meet him at the cross where we are cherished, I was pridefully trying to live without him.

To be in need every day, every hour…that's painful to pride. It's hard to accept. It's so easy to want to do something significant in order to *be* someone significant, but that way of thinking is a mirage. First we *become* significant in Christ, and then we *do* out of thankfulness.

I misunderstood the cross. It seemed like a place of personal humiliation where God rubbed my face in my failures, instead of a place where I could be fed, healed, loved, and rejoiced over. It was the place where I saw deep, never-ending disappointment in Jesus' eyes, instead of a place where he looked at me with delight, a place where I could grow in an intimate relationship with him.

He does show us our sin, but only to bless us. He didn't save us to then condemn us, or to abandon us in our struggles against sin; rather, we continue to come as we first did: we repent, turn, and are welcomed with never-ending love.

I spent a lot of years asking God not to give up on me, that I would get it right and some day stop disappointing him. When Dave got sick, I mercifully came to the end of myself. I finally realized I had nothing to give, and then God was glorified.

> We strive against God's all-sufficient glory if we think we can become a means to his end without making joy in him our end…It is precisely in confessing our frustrated, hopeless condition without him that we honor him…the one who actually sets himself above God is the person who presumes to come to God to give rather than get. With a pretense of self-denial he positions himself as God's benefactor.[38]
>
> ~ John Piper

~ *Day 61* ~

"Now we see but a poor reflection as in a mirror; then we shall see face to face. Now I know in part; then I shall know fully, even as I am fully known."

~ 1 Corinthians 13:12

"I'm tired of being in the box of mirrors, where I'm always looking at myself," a friend said to me. She feared the trials that might come but perhaps the most painful one of all would be to escape that box.

When the walls of pride are shattered, the shards may wound us on the way out. But it will not break us, because selfishness is not *of* us any more, now that we have a new nature. Selfishness finds its way into us and needs to be purged, but is no longer what defines us.

It is a reflection of what we were, not the substance of what we are. It is an illusion, and as reflection mirrors reflection, it is confusing, misleading, taunting, but it is not who we are now. We have to take our eyes off the reflections that seem so clear, and look to the dim reflection of our true reality.

When we come out of the box, we leave behind that former cocoon of pride and selfishness and put on love and a desire for God to be glorified. The way out is not to look at our own reflection, but at his.

Each week at my church we read a prayer of confession, and then remember the Lord's mercy and grace. This simple habit of going to the cross feeds our souls and shows his face.

What we see in this life may be a poor reflection, but it's still a wonderful gift. We see the back of his head as Moses and Elijah did—we see his hand and where he's been. We see grace and love in Jesus. Do we look for that glimpse of his face that one day we shall know fully, even as we are fully known? ✍

Lean Back

Do you want to see God? Go to the cross. It's only at the cross that we see our true selves: hungry, thirsty, empty, naked, blind, wretched, poor, desperately in need of forgiveness, mercy, love—in need of the lifeblood of the savior to flow through our veins.

Whose reflection have you been looking at? For many years I believed, but thought of God as un-seeable, un-touchable—virtually un-knowable. And then God began to change me through Dave's illness. He wooed me and captured my heart.

The cross isn't merely a one-time event that we move on from. It's a vast ocean that we haven't even begun to plumb the depths of; it's our eternal source of life, freedom, and joy. It's the place God where God meets us continually, fills us, and reveals himself. He shows us our sin not to pound in our unworthiness, but to be merciful, to show overabundant grace.

Maybe God is using your circumstance to change you as well. Maybe he's calling you to cross that Jordan to a new freedom, to fathom the joys of union with him.

"Therefore I am now going to allure her;
I will lead her into the desert and speak tenderly to her.
There I will give her back her vineyards
and will make the Valley of Achor a door of hope.
There she will sing as in the days of her youth,
as in the day she came up out of Egypt.
"In that day," declares the LORD,
"you will call me 'my husband';
You will no longer call me 'my master.'
I will betroth you to me forever;
I will betroth you in righteousness and justice,
in love and compassion.
I will betroth you in faithfulness,
and you will acknowledge the LORD."

~ Hosea 2:14-16, 19-20 ∽

Chapter Ten

GOD, HOW MUCH MORE?
The Power of an Indestructible Life

*I know that my Redeemer lives, and that in the
end he will stand on the earth. And after my skin
has been destroyed, yet in my flesh I will see God;
I myself will see him with my own eyes—I and not
another. How my heart yearns within me.*

~ Job 19:25-27

~ *Day 62* ~

...The poor will see and be glad—
you who seek God, may your hearts live!"

~ Psalm 69: 32

The lure of seeing God spurred me on. The pain, the disease, our crazy lives, the insurance battles all waged war on me; they were beyond my ability to endure. But I was on a journey to see God, to see his face, to find my strength in him.

There is hope in relying on God. If we rely on ourselves, we are over-burdened—that suitcase is too full. When we rely on God, we acknowledge that it's too much for us, but we are not defeated—we have hope! Hope in God is different from hope in being rescued from difficulties. It is an attitude we choose based on eternity rather than emotions or circumstances.

The American Heritage dictionary defines emotion as a strong, subjective response. Attitude, on the other hand, refers to position. For an aircraft, attitude is the orientation of its axes to a reference line, like the horizon.[39] Jesus is our reference line, the one who keeps us level. Our emotions and circumstances may roller coaster, but our attitude remains the same. Romans 5:2 says, "our hope is in the glory of God." If strong emotions like fear or anger rule us, we will roller coaster with them. If in these emotions we fix our eyes on him, we remain steadfast, and find protection, rest, and refuge.

We stand as wind, earthquakes, and fire tear our lives apart, but he is in the gentle whisper. We hear him if we are listening, and we see him if we are looking. The view on the mountain is terrifying, electrifying, riveting—and necessary to behold his glory. "Be still," he calls to us. That's how we hear a whisper. Humility, reliance on God, relinquishing self—that's how we see his face. That is God's calling to us.

Sometimes we see. Sometimes the battle rages on. ✎

~ *Day 63* ~

O LORD, you deceived me, and I was deceived;
You overpowered me and prevailed.

~ Jeremiah 20:7a

Journal from the first winter:

I vacillate between crying and being too empty to cry. Anticipation of life's little joys is now futile, and the memories left behind are painful. Crying through church alone, imagining the children's Christmas program, wishing we could sit together. Dave couldn't even be around us when we came home. The scent of others' perfume gave him a headache, and he had to lie down.

I am so alone, and I belong nowhere. Dave is no longer "staff," I am not a "Pastor's wife," and people don't know what to do with me. My mind feels like it will burst every day. I have aged a year in the last month. A decade has squeezed into one small year, and wrung out every drop of life that I had to offer.

Dave had a couple of good days this week. But today I thought he was going to pull out his central line for his IV meds. He said he didn't like it and didn't want it. He knows he's not thinking right.

My world is so far from reality. My mind searches for what's sane, and I struggle with completing my thoughts. But with my dear, interrupting toddler and preschooler, and a husband who interrupts just as much—how can I not tend them with love, how can I think I should not be interrupted?

I find myself wondering if people think I'm making things up. Our life doesn't sound real to me anymore. I just keep living and hope one day the nightmare will be over.

I look around at the things undone in the house, and find it hard to care. I eat, not because I'm hungry, but because there is something to put into me. It doesn't satisfy; I just keep eating. I stay up late and neglect myself. I live only to put out fires:

There's an insurance fire, put it out! Write the letters. There's a kid fire, put it out! Feed the child! Hug the child! And hug the child some more because there is nothing else to do. Sometimes we laugh, and it feels good because it's so foreign. There's a husband fire, make the meds! Get the pain pill! Something's perfumy, wash it! Get rid of it! And when I've put out these fires, I return to the emergency within, the anguish that sees no end.

Anna begs to be held, and I don't know how much this all is hurting her. Zach pretends he's sick all the time. I want to run away, but everyone's pain would be greater if I did that.

Sometimes Dave cries out in pain and holds his wrists or ribs— last night it hurt so much he was crying. It reminds me of the pain my father went through with kidney disease, and I am as helpless now as I was then. We never stop being a child in many ways.

People ask me how Dave is and the words betray me; nothing can explain what we have been through. If only I was Anna, I wouldn't have words but would communicate my whole heart with my cries, and then people would see I am inconsolable, that the pain knows no end.

Sometimes when I'm holding her it's as if I am her, being held by another who is holding me, consoling me, being my security, my stronghold, my safety. She is a gift deeper than words can say, and great healing is in her. As it is in Zach who seems to know how to say an encouraging word at just the right time.

The length of our days is seventy years—
or eighty, if we have the strength;
yet their span is but trouble and sorrow,
for they quickly pass, and we fly away.
Relent, O Lord! How long will it be?
Have compassion on your servants.
Satisfy us in the morning with your unfailing love,
that we may sing for joy and be glad all our days.
Make us glad for as many days as you have afflicted us,
for as many years as we have seen trouble.

~ Psalm 90:10, 13-15 ∾

~ *Day 64* ~

I am worn out calling for help; my throat is parched.
My eyes fail, looking for my God

~ Psalm 69:3

I was done.

The breaking in my heart seemed unending. I found anger, raw emotion, vulnerability, emptiness, longing, and loneliness that was too profound to describe with words.

I felt like I lived in two worlds—the world of the healthy, and the world of the sick, and I didn't know who I was any more. When I went to a mom's group or AWANA or some-one's house, everything seemed surreal. Their life, what I used to consider normal, was not normal to me anymore. It seemed foreign, unattainable, unnatural. My life also seemed abnormal, endless, and even meaningless.

That first winter was relentless with its snow—36" in a month! And life seemed relentless with its time, it just came and came and came, and I couldn't shovel it all away.

I wanted to die. I wouldn't end my life because I didn't want to cause more pain for others, I couldn't do that to my family and friends. Still, I wished the nightmare would end.

What do we do with pain beyond description, beyond words, that is too much to bear? Who will bear it with us, and how, when it's beyond bearing, do we rely on God? Where do we find God's love, and how can we be safe and protected?

One night I asked God, *"What are your intentions towards Dave?"* I had prayed all along that God would not drag this out, but would either take Dave home to him, or bring him home to me. God answered my question with a question: what were *my* intentions were towards Dave? What if Dave never got better, and never got worse, but stayed just as he was right then, what would I do? I realized my intention was to love him even if he couldn't love me back the same way, even if we couldn't communicate or share as we used to.

God asked me to relinquish everything I needed and desired to him, and let him do with it what he willed. And he gave me in their place the great opportunity to agape-love Dave, without necessarily receiving back. The kind of love Dave had shown me so many times through his selfless, giving, servant's heart. How God has humbled me through the love of this man, and how he humbles me now because I know Dave longs for Christ glorified.

Love reaches us in the places where the pain of life wounds. Do enough of us care about our fellow man to love? Do we visit the poor, the sick, the elderly, do we care for the homeless, the destitute, do we think about those who may, right now, be wishing to die because to go on living seems too harsh, too impossible, too incredibly painful? If we are able, we should do this—perhaps especially in remembrance of those who cannot.

But if one cannot—there is no shame in what we cannot do. Only use what we have, little or much, to his glory. He will greatly multiply even a mustard seed or a widow's mite. If you are drained and have nothing to give, then collapse in the arms of our loving Bridegroom. You are not less than. He gave all to purchase you, redeem you. He gave all to become one with you and call you his own. You are his beloved, and nothing will ever change that.

> Who shall separate us from the love of Christ? Shall trouble or hardship or persecution or famine or nakedness or danger or sword?...For I am convinced that neither death nor life, neither angels nor demons, neither the present nor the future, or any powers, neither height nor depth, nor anything else in all creation will be able to separate us from the love of God that is in Christ Jesus our Lord.
>
> ~Romans 8:35, 38-39

~ *Day 65* ~

To live is Christ and to die is gain.

~ Philippians 1:21

The winter days continued bleak and dark. We kept the lights low when Dave was awake. He forgot where he was at times, and wondered why there was snow in the "summer." His fog was frightening.

Paul says, "to live is Christ and to die is gain." In my heart I thought to live is worse than death but to choose death is worse than life. I felt trapped, powerless, like there was no way out.

For weeks Satan tried in every way to convince me that life was destructible and that I should view it in such a way. I really wanted a way to just end my life without hurting others, and realizing there was no way to do that made me feel trapped. The oppression was suffocating. And then God gave me air to breathe in these verses about Jesus:

> ...one who has become a priest not on the basis of a regulation as to his ancestry but on the basis of the power of an indestructible life...
>
> ~ Hebrews 7:16

I was blown away because I realized that since Jesus is in me, then this power of an indestructible life is in me, and I could rest in that power. Something more powerful than my emotions, peace that passes understanding! And since we are *in Christ*—this peace is a sure refuge. I began praying that God would fill me with the power of an indestructible life so that I wouldn't want to destroy mine.

God gave me real freedom here because I realized, I DID have choices—I wasn't trapped! I didn't have to obey my feelings (that were telling me to run away or destroy myself), I was to obey God.

We are not powerless. Jesus is our priest on the basis of the power of an indestructible life—an immense power to overcome immense pain. On our own we drum up despair, depression, thoughts of death—and he comes to save us with life-giving power. The lie of Satan is that we are cornered with only one way out. God offers us the ability to walk through the flames and come out more beautiful. God enables us to choose life over death, and to choose love over bitterness. We are weak, but his power rescues us. He is the better hope by which we draw near to God.

Father, I pray for those hurting right now. Oh God we need you! You alone know the depth of pain, anguish, the struggles and trials—for you have been with us and wept with us and struggled with us. Lord, come to our rescue and bring the freedom we need, show us the choices we have to be set free from this trapped feeling. Let us know the truth that you delight in us. In Jesus' name, amen. ❧

~ *Day 66* ~

"He rescued me from my powerful enemy, from my foes, who were too strong for me. They confronted me in the day of my disaster, but the LORD was my support. He brought me out into a spacious place; he rescued me because he delighted in me."

~ Psalm 18:17-19

How do we battle thoughts of death, enemies named despair and hopelessness? With the power of an indestructible life! *Jesus saves us!* His amazing, life-giving power gives us strength.

Journal from the next spring:

I will choose to continue on. I choose courage, I choose life, I choose to love my husband and family and God, I choose to shun bitterness, I choose to find joy and meaning when I can. It is a daily choice and a daily struggle and sometimes a daily hell because the memories are strong, and the desires are powerful. The beauty of what I expected from life is hard to turn away from, because it clings to me with its many tentacles. I have to take it off each day and learn what it means to rely on God and fix my eyes on Jesus in a way I never conceived or expected to need to do.

I have to exchange my goals for God's, and relinquish my will in every area; I never considered that that would be required of me. If I didn't have God I would only be relinquishing it to the futility of disease and the hope of what this world has to offer. But I have a better hope, that God will bring something good out of a meaningless tragedy. Pain has met the power of an indestructible life, and this world cannot change me in any way that God does not will; I am in his hands and his power works mightily in me.

Pain has met the Power of an Indestructible Life, full on, face to face—and God calls us to fix our eyes on him. ๑

Lean Back

"Surely no more terrible abyss can be conceived," writes Calvin, "than to feel yourself forsaken and estranged from God; and when you call upon him not to be heard." It should be a comfort to us in our torment that there is no hell we can face greater than the one Christ endured; that there is no one better to sympathize with our hellish moments than Christ; and that there is no one else able to save us from the wrath of God than He who has faced it already.[40]

—Kevin DeYoung

Have you come to a place where you can't see how to go on? Please, tell someone. You need a plan when destructive thoughts come, and someone to call day or night, to be with you and help you when you are discouraged. Someone who will tell you honestly when you may need to call a pastor or counselor or doctor. Don't go through this alone—and don't let pride tell you that you can do it on your own. I had my pastor, doctor, counselor, friends, family, and church whose prayer, support, and counsel were an incredible source of strength for me. I know it was through their prayers that God led me to the truth of Hebrews 7:16:

The power of an indestructible life

His love endures forever—Psalm 107:1

His faithfulness reaches to the skies—Psalm 108:4

His righteousness endures forever—Psalm 111:3

His salvation lasts forever—Isaiah 51:6

His covenant is everlasting—Ezekiel 37:26

He betroths us to him forever—Hosea 2:19

He puts his Name on us forever—1 Kings 9:3

His sanctuary is among us forever—Ezekiel 37:26

He lives with us forever—2 John 2

He will swallow up death forever—Isaiah 25:8

He reigns forever—Psalm 9:7

He gives us his Holy Spirit forever—John 14:6

His word stands forever—1 Peter 1:25

He remembers his covenant forever—Psalm 111:5

He is a priest forever, he has sworn!—Hebrews 7:21

Imagine—Jesus never, *ever* stops interceding for you, his beloved, his delight. He uses the greatest, most extraordinary power that exists on our behalf, to be our priest, our intercessor, our guarantee, our hope. He could condemn us and instead betroths us and unites us with him.

Indestructible life. Forever. That is the surety, the rock, of his covenant with us.

His mighty power encouraged me in my darkest days, and I pray that you also will draw strength from his power. ✂

Part Three

BEHOLD OUR BELOVED
God Pours Out His Love

Brokenness is realizing God is all I have
Hope is realizing God is all I need
Joy is realizing God is all I want[41]

~ Larry Crabb

"I will be glad and rejoice in your love,
for you saw my affliction
and knew the anguish of my soul."

~ Psalm 31:7

Chapter Eleven

DYING TO SEE HIM
Submitting Brings Joy

Those who sow in tears
will reap with songs of joy.
He who goes out weeping,
carrying seed to sow,
will return with songs of joy,
carrying sheaves with him.

~ Psalm 126:5-6

~ *Day 67* ~

...God has chosen to make known among the
Gentiles the glorious riches of this mystery,
which is Christ in you, the hope of glory.

~ Colossians 1:27

The Waterfall was back on the wall! The nail we used to hang Dave's IV bag was empty for several days before I remembered to re-hang the picture. The picture beckoned me with the quiet strength of its powerful waters, to trust God and his timing in Dave's life and mine.

Dave still wasn't well. It felt like giving up to have to stop the IV. *God, why didn't you work things out and provide the insurance? How will Dave get well?* But the picture was a reminder to look beyond what I can readily see—myself and my world—and look to God.

For since the creation of the world God's invisible
qualities— his eternal power and divine nature—
have been clearly seen, being understood from
what has been made, so that men are without
excuse.

~ Romans 1:20

Clearly seen! The Power of an Indestructible Life, The Great I Am, the Everlasting Father, the Prince of Peace is living within us. Immanuel, God with us—that great name that protects us[42]—the name nothing can conquer—its power is so great that nothing can separate us from our God.[43] Nothing. That is an incredible promise. Christ in you, the hope of glory—God is intimately seeking us.

I keep asking that the God of our Lord Jesus
Christ, the glorious Father, may give you the
Spirit of wisdom and revelation, so that you may
know him better.

~ Ephesians 1:17 ∞

~ *Day 68* ~

> ...And we rejoice in the hope of the glory of God.
> Not only so, but we also rejoice in our sufferings,
> because we know that suffering produces perse-
> verance; perseverance, character; and character,
> hope. And hope does not disappoint us because
> God has poured out his love into our hearts by
> the Holy Spirit, whom he has given us.
>
> ~ Romans 5:2b-5

Our journey through these chapters has traced Romans 5. Perseverance is often walking without seeing. We continue on even when there is no visible hope of God. What we can readily see—ourselves, illness, troubles—does not triumph. We wrestle as Jacob did and don't let go. We persevere to know God, to stand in his presence as Job did and meet God face to face. To continually seek his presence and refuse to be satisfied with less.

Character is a deep trust in God, submitting willingly. Character directs our hope past the things of this world that we can easily see, to a deeper sight, to joyous hope dependent on a promise—and thus it is a hope that can be fulfilled. Our hope is a deepening longing to see God and see him glorified.

And this hope does not disappoint because God pours out his love into our hearts. Our hope is secure. When we choose to walk with God through the pain of suffering, we gain the eyes that behold him. The power of an indestructible life in us meets the pain face to face, so we can be filled by our incredible God.

Is God worth the relinquishing of our health, our ability to give to others and do for ourselves? If that is the only choice before us, then it is a holy calling, and yes, he is worthy. We relinquish our bodies and minds and souls, our hearts and wishes, dreams and desires, to the ever-loving, ever-merciful, ever-open arms of God. We die to self and say, *I am yours, do with me as you choose.* ೫

~ *Day 69* ~

Those who sow in tears
will reap with songs of joy.
He who goes out weeping,
carrying seed to sow,
will return with songs of joy,
carrying sheaves with him.

~ Psalm 126:5-6

It had never occurred to me in Dave's illness that I might be "carrying seed to sow," as Psalm 126 says, or that there was a harvest to reap, other than more sorrow and heartache. How do we attain this harvest of joy? And what miraculous seed do we sow in tears that it could return so utterly changed in its very nature, as to become joy?

Yet, that is the nature of planting and harvesting. We plant a seed but something very different grows in its place. A change of such magnitude is almost unfathomable, yet we often take it for granted. Can we fully understand the process? We can learn the botanical names and stages, and even predict what will happen, but where does the power come from for a seed to become an abundant harvest?

"I tell you the truth, unless a kernel of wheat falls to the ground and dies, it remains only a single seed. But if it dies, it produces many seeds. The man who loves his life will lose it, while the man who hates his life in this world will keep it for eternal life."

~ John 12:24-25

The seed has to die.

A seed is a powerful thing—it contains life, the imprint of something unimaginable from just looking at it. What is in our seed? Our dreams, hopes, fears, desires—all we are or hope to be, identity, self-will.... God has called us to drop it to the ground and let it die. Not merely because we desire something—sometimes what we desire happens to coincide with what God desires. No, it's because "I no longer live, but Christ lives in me" (Galatians 2:20). We die to self so that Christ's life can spring forth.

Jesus often said that he did nothing on his own—that all he said and did came from the Father. This is who we are now called to be. A seed, falling to the ground, dying. Dormant in the dark, cold ground until the miraculous power of God brings something new, totally unlike the seed and yet from the seed—fruit, beautiful fruit. ❧

~ *Day 70* ~

> If you obey my commands, you will remain in my
> love, just as I have obeyed my Father's com-
> mands and remain in his love. I have told you
> this so that my joy may be in you and that your
> joy may be complete.
>
> ~ John 15:10-11

The seed we sow is the seed of obedience, the death to self. Jesus promises that if we obey his commands, we remain in his love, and his joy will be in us, and that *joy will be complete!*

What are we to obey? Jesus said the greatest commandment is to "Love the Lord your God with all your heart and with all your soul and with all your mind and with all your strength." That requires time. Time spent in his Word so that we can know him, his character and his promises. Time spent in pray- er—in talking things over with him but also in listening to him, allowing him to give us a deeper understanding of his Word.

And then Jesus said the second commandment is like it, to "Love your neighbor as yourself" (Mark 12:30-31). That re- quires time spent with other people: caring, looking for their needs, listening—not merely staying busy with programs, al- though there are lots of good programs out there. It can be easy, though to take on too many activities and experience burnout instead of joy. Instead, in whatever way, great or small, find some way to be involved in simply loving others. Enjoying one another. Enjoying God! 🙠

~ *Day 71* ~

The precepts of the LORD are right,
giving joy to the heart.
The commands of the LORD are radiant,
giving light to the eyes.

~ Psalm 19:8

It's easy to assume that obedience leads to drudgery, disappointment and confinement. This is what the father of lies would have us believe. But joy often relates to obedience, to delighting in God's laws, and fearing or revering God. The "fear of the Lord is the beginning of wisdom" (Proverbs 9:10).

The Psalmist says to ascribe to the Lord the glory and honor and power due his name (Psalm 29). That his wrath is as great as the fear that is due him (Psalm 90:11). Revelation 14:7 says to fear God and give him glory. Luke 1:50 promises, "His mercy extends to those who fear him, from generation to generation."

If we don't embrace the full truth of God's sovereignty, that we belong to him and are his to do with as he wills—if we don't die to self, we won't ever know joy, the powerful protection he extends around us, or the greatest peace that exists.

God's sovereignty and authority is like no other—though he has the right to make us slaves, he embraces us as children and calls us friends. A friend is trustworthy, and can be brought into one's confidence. The more we are about fulfilling God's will, the more he can reveal to us what his will is.

Why are God's statutes, commands, and laws the delight of the Psalmists? Because they reveal the truth of God's character. They are a window to God's soul. They allow us to see the depth of his love, the firmness of his justice, the beauty of his mercy, the glory of his wisdom, the winsomeness of his ways. We relinquish ourselves to God to *see him.* ☜

~ *Day 72* ~

Whoever has my commands and obeys them, he
is the one who loves me. He who loves me will be
loved by my Father, and I too will love him and
show myself to him.

~ John 14:21

Are you longing for God to show himself to you? Obey
him. Even more, be holy as he is holy. At first, this might seem
impossible, but here again, God provides for us.

One of the hardest sections of the Bible for me is Hebrews
12, which says we are to endure hardship as discipline—God is
treating us as sons. I can feel the hair start to bristle on the back
of my neck, but then I command pride to die again, take a deep
breath and ask, why? And God replies with this gem in the
same chapter: *So we can share in his holiness.* "Without holiness
no one will see God" (Hebrews 12:14b). And this is the point
we often miss. We think, be Holy because it's commanded, it's
about right and wrong. And so being right becomes our focus
instead of Christ.

Christ died so we could rest from our efforts to achieve sin-
less perfection, so that we could labor in love, motivated by our
devotion to and rich communion with him. As we look to him,
he works in us and changes us. But we often get caught up in
looking at what needs to be changed in us, instead of being
consumed by him, by his glory and grace, by his passion for us.

Holiness means different from. God has set us apart (sancti-
fied us) to be different from (holy) the world. What God has
declared us to be (holy) in Christ, we are now learning to be—
just as we declare a couple married and then they spend a lifetime learning how to be married.

God is teaching us, one step at a time, how to be what he
has called us. He has made us holy so we can see him, and he is
making us holy as we look at him, so we can see him more. ✍

~ *Day 73* ~

...The joy of the LORD is your strength.

~ Nehemiah 8:10

How are we different from the world? How can we "be holy as he is holy?" We look to the suffering of Christ and let that mold our hearts in every way as we go through our own suffering. By his strength we can love when we are treated unfairly. We can be patient when we suffer. We look to the needs of others and not only ourselves—sometimes at great, personal cost. We sacrifice without seeking personal gain. And just as Christ endured "for the joy set before him" (Hebrews 12:2), so we also look to joy as our strength.

What does this mean? When I have joy I feel stronger, I'm able to face and deal with life. When I am grieving or sorrowful, I feel as though each additional burden is too much; I am depleted, deflated—I have no strength. Taking joy in God requires trust which brings peace.

Here in Nehemiah 8 we find the word sacred paired with joy, similar to revere and joy in other verses. They declared that the day was sacred, and that was why they should not grieve. How do these go together?

Revere somehow goes beyond trust, as a more intense or deeper concept. Sacred means set aside to God instead of set aside to ourselves.

There is a time for grief—Jesus himself wept and the Holy Spirit grieves. But there is also a time for joy in the Lord—to let grief be silent because the day is sacred. A time to recognize and remember, all things are in his hands—it will be okay. He is using even this to help us see him. ∞

~ *Day 74* ~

The name of the LORD is a strong tower;
The righteous run to it and are safe.

~ Proverbs 18:10

The name of the Lord, the sum of who God is, is a strong tower. In him we look down and see that we don't need what the world seeks; we trust him to meet our needs because we bear his name. Joy knows safety and security—the strong tower.

Joy knows the Lord is near; it comes from his presence.

Joy in him brings thankfulness—and without thankfulness I am weakened by needs or desires.

It brings peace—without peace I am weakened by anxiety.

Joy includes endurance, hope, and faith.

Joy may be to man as big a word as Grace is to God. Grace is the fullness of God's glory; joy in the Lord reflects that glory.

Joy is our radiance from God through Christ living in and through us—and more and more as we die to self.

Romans 5 lists *rejoice* first, though it is also the culmination of God's work in our lives. Joy looks back (perseverance) and looks ahead (hope) and lives now (character). Perhaps the deeper the suffering, the deeper the joy he can bring, if we are willing—the beatitudes. Blessed are those who mourn, the poor in spirit, those who hunger and thirst for righteousness.

> Though the fig tree does not bud and there are no grapes on the vines, though the olive crop fails and the fields produce no food, though there are no sheep in the pen and no cattle in the stalls, yet I will rejoice in the LORD, I will be joyful in God my Savior. The Sovereign LORD is my strength; he makes my feet like the feet of a deer, he enables me to go on the heights.

~ *Habakkuk 3:17-19* ✍

Lean Back

"Delight yourself in the Lord and he will give you the desires of your heart" (Psalm 37:4). Nothing else can make this promise. I love chocolate, and ice cream, and together even better. My favorite kind has ribbons of chocolate fudge and mini chocolate peanut butter cups. When I eat it, I am definitely experiencing happiness. But it cannot give me the desires of my heart, because I desire to eat as much of it as I want whenever I want, and to be thin, and to not spend all of my money on ice cream. And if I forego the desires to be thin and save money, I would eventually make myself sick on it. So, one way or another, there is a limit, a boundary, an end.

Not so with God. In him, we can have complete and full joy, with no boundaries, no limits. The more we enjoy him, the more of him we discover to enjoy.

Dying to self is a frightening thought. Submitting to God's sovereignty can seem terrifying. But there we find rest, security, and joy. There we see God. We so easily give up on pursuing God but there is so much of God to know. He is endless.

And just imagine—God took 6 days to create the earth. But he has been making a home for us for about 2000 years. What is he doing? Think on the possibilities!

He came for you. He died for you. Do you know how passionate he is for you, how he put himself at risk to protect, care, and provide for you? Your Bridegroom has gone to prepare a place, and will one day return for his bride! ❧

Chapter Twelve

AWESTRUCK BY HIS PRESENCE
Developing Night-Vision

*Where is God when it hurts? For whatever reason,
God has chosen to respond to our predicament not by
waving a magic wand to make evil and suffering dis-
appear, but by joining us and absorbing it in his very
person.*[44]

~ *Philip Yancey*

~ *Day 75* ~

You, O LORD, keep my lamp burning;
my God turns my darkness into light.

~ Psalm 18:28

When our world is filled with darkness, do we turn to God for light? Do we run into the strong tower of his name, do we expect God to show himself? Have we stopped to contemplate his love until the honor of his attention and the gentleness of his care overwhelms us?

> The mystery is that God is not so much the object of our knowledge as the cause of our wonder. The mystery is that I shall never know God exhaustively yet I may know sufficient to feel compelled to fall at his feet in wonder, love and praise. The mystery is that he is both hidden and revealed.45

~ Joyce Huggett

Her words have encouraged me to contemplate God in a new way. It's so easy to unknowingly simplify God in our finite minds and think we know him, when we will spend an eternity getting to know God. Have we lost the mystery of marveling at God? Have we let go the art of contemplating God, of thirsting for him?

Sometimes we have only glimpses of God seeming real, and long, dry stretches of being empty and lonely—not that our relationship with God is about what we feel. But there are times that prayer feels more like talking *at* God than considering that God might want to talk to us.

Even so God is gracious and longs to reveal himself to us more than we long to know him. He is a personal God who draws us with love and kindness—he is to be known. It's so simple-sounding that almost any Christian would say, "I know that." But it is such a deep mystery to experience God, to walk into his presence with confidence and reverence and awe and overcome with love and thankfulness, wearing joy as our crown. *"How do I do that?"* I have asked God.

There is no certain outcome for late-stage Lyme. I choose not to rest my hope in the possibility of changing circumstances. Instead I seek to rise to the challenge of putting my hope in the character of God, in knowing him who pours out his love into our hearts, the hope that grows all the more while hope in the world fades away. It's a challenge, and I don't claim to have achieved proficiency in this, but it's what I strive for. It's my sustenance, a choice food that God has given me a taste of; I want more of him.

> On Good Friday Jesus absorbed the worst of what Earth has to offer, a convergence of evil and death in an event of profound injustice.[46]
>
> ~Philip Yancey

He knows. More than any other, he understands our pain. God is good, loving, sovereign, trustworthy, true, faithful, kind, everlasting, king, supreme, gracious, mighty, strong, all-knowing, all-powerful—and for some reason has chosen to make his dwelling with man. Do we know the mystery, the awe and reverence, do we marvel at his majesty and intimacy with us? Do we kneel before him in adoration and amazement? Do we meet him at the cross and bow in submission and trust? If we are to do this, then we must know him personally, intimately, reverently, with confidence and perseverance.

> "God did this so that men would seek him and perhaps reach out for him and find him, though he is not far from each one of us."
>
> ~ Acts 17:27 ☙

~ *Day 76* ~

When darkness seems to hide His face,
I rest on His unchanging grace.
In every high and stormy gale,
my anchor holds within the vale.

His oath, His covenant, His blood
support me in the whelming flood.
When all around my soul gives way,
He then is all my Hope and Stay.

When He shall come with trumpet sound,
Oh, may I then in him be found;
Dressed in His righteousness alone,
faultless to stand before the throne.[47]

~ Edward Mote

My concept of prayer has changed dramatically. When Dave was first sick, my idea of prayer had at its core the desire to manipulate God into doing my will. I coveted the prayers of others because I felt I did not have that kind of clout with God, but thought maybe I could find someone who did. But I also felt certain that God had something else in mind, and that he wanted me to have something else in mind as well.

I wondered, *What good is prayer if it's not the magic tool to getting my own way?* I decided, *if God won't do what I want, what can I pray that he will answer?* God knows Dave has Lyme. I have no new information to give God, and no new rationalization for why my way is good that God hasn't thought of. Yet he wants us to seek him and bring our requests to him, why?

We pray not to fulfill our own plans—though sometimes what we want is also what God has in mind. We pray so we can know him! To talk to him, learn of him, and seek his face. We need to stop talking the importance of prayer and start praying.

In *Fresh Wind, Fresh Fire,* Jim Cymbala quotes a visiting pastor: "You can tell how popular Jesus is by who comes to the prayer meeting." In another place he says, "If we don't want to experience God's closeness here on earth, why would we want to go to heaven?"[48]

As I was growing up, my concept of heaven was merely one of comfort and convenience—no more tears, sickness, trouble. But glorious heaven is so much more! It is to be in the Presence of God himself! Do we want to be with him? This is the essence of prayer.

My prayers have changed. *Make me like Jesus. Give me courage to follow you no matter what, boldness to speak of you, love to serve you, love for those around me, and wisdom to discern what is best. Open my eyes to you. Make my attitude patient like Jesus, loving, not self-serving. Soften my heart that I might be moldable, not proud or stubborn. Heal Dave, but if not, be glorified in whatever you do.*

When I pray now, I am often consumed by his holiness, the awesomeness of his presence. I have a reverence for him that I didn't have before.

When was the last time we were overwhelmed by his holiness, fell to our knees, repented in dust and ashes, and asked him to take the coal to our lips? When was the last time you went into the Holy of Holies and felt the perfect peace of him wrapping his wing around you in protection and love?

What I wanted was the power to change God's mind, to move God to the action I desired. What I find instead is that prayer is changing my mind, my heart, my desires, and my attitude.

Prayer is not power over God but submission to God. Maybe God allows trials in our lives so that we can know his sovereignty, seek his face on our knees, learn the joy of his presence, and the holiness of his rest. ✠

~ *Day 77* ~

Oh Jerusalem, Jerusalem, how I longed to draw
you into my wings like a hen does her chicks, but
you were not willing!

~ Luke 13:34

I think it's easy to shrug off what God is offering: his Presence. Like Jerusalem, God is longing to draw us near, to protect us in his wings, but we would not. His command offered protection to Adam and Eve, and they shrugged it off for what looked good in their own eyes. Understanding does not begin in our judgment, but in God's—which is why the fear of God is the beginning of wisdom.

We lost part of the protection of God in our world, and we live with the result—a world plagued with horror and disease and the atrocities of what one man does to another. Some people consider these things to be evidence that there is no God. However, I think Thomas Merton's view is closer to the truth:

It is only the infinite mercy and love of God that
has prevented us from tearing ourselves to
pieces and destroying his entire creation long
ago. People seem to think that it is in some way
a proof that no merciful God exists, if we have so
many wars. On the contrary, consider how in
spite of centuries of sin and greed and lust and
cruelty and hatred and avarice and oppression
and injustice, spawned and bred by the free wills
of men, the human race can still recover, each
time, and can still produce men and women who
overcome evil with good, hatred with love, greed
with charity, lust and cruelty with sanctity. How
could all this be possible without the merciful love
of God, pouring out his grace upon us?[49]

Creation and destruction, love and hatred, live side by side in our world—God is showing himself, a light in the darkness. Are we looking for him?

God has protected man throughout the ages by always ensuring there is a remnant that follows him. We have no way of knowing how many things God really does spare us from in his mercy. He lets us see the full extent of sin, the darkness of evil, how awful it is to live without God—and to develop the night-vision that enables us to realize he is our only protection and hope. His desire is that we will allow him to draw us near, to shelter us in his wings, to receive his love.

"He is the treasure we seek...the precious gem to be mined. Have you heard his whispers?" asks Joni Eareckson Tada[50]. This world is full of many kinds of hell. God is our only hope of deliverance from all of our trials, physical and spiritual.

Because you are my help,
I sing in the shadow of your wings.
My soul clings to you;
your right hand upholds me.

~ Psalm 63:7-8 ∞

~ *Day 78* ~

Be merciful to me, O LORD, for I am in distress;
my eyes grow weak with sorrow,
my soul and my body with grief.
My life is consumed by anguish and my years by groaning;
my strength fails because of my affliction,
and my bones grow weak.

~ Psalm 31:9-10

Sometimes my faith falters and I think, "God's not helping me, he's not protecting us!" One night when I was really struggling, I came across an excerpt from Doris Van Stone's *No Place to Cry*. Doris was repeatedly physically and sexually abused as a child:

> "God did not shield me from the violations of my body, yet I still clung to him, believing that He would be with me. He gave me the grace to bear my trials. That's why I have never been bitter or angry with my heavenly Father. It was He who chose me to belong to him; He who led those students to the orphanage to tell me about God's love... Someday I shall speak to my Savior, who stood with me when no one else did."[51]

Doris had night-vision beyond comprehension. Despite the agony that she went through, she found peace that passes understanding. She knew the One who guards our hearts and minds in Christ Jesus (Philippians 4:7).

At such horrendous times, God doesn't turn his back on us; he weeps with us and lives through the horror with us. He is infuriated, and has established a Judgment Day for those who commit such heinous acts. We long for the justice only he is powerful enough to bring, and he will storm down and bring it.

But for the *power* of his Spirit living in us, who could stand in this hell, this war-zone world? He will bring us home. ∞

~ *Day 79* ~

O LORD, the God who saves me,
day and night I cry out before you.
May my prayer come before you;
turn your ear to my cry,
For my soul is full of trouble
and my life draws near the grave.
...Why, O LORD, do you reject me
and hide your face from me?
...the darkness is my closest friend.

~ Psalm 88:1-3, 14, 18

"Jesus was heard," we read triumphantly in Hebrews 5:7, "because of his reverent submission." Yet there he hangs, bleeding, searing pain, dying on the cross—forsaken by God.

> In that darkest of nights that fell upon his soul, Christ pleaded for mercy that wasn't granted, encountered suffering he didn't deserve, asked questions that went unanswered. Even so, he surrendered his will, his rights, his very life into the hands of his heavenly Father, however painful it was to do so.[52]
>
> ~ Ken Gire

He "learned obedience through what he suffered." He could say the words, "not my will..." but now he lived them. He was heard, and God's answer was to give him strength,[53] and then afterward, "being in anguish, he prayed more earnestly...."

God gives us the ability, like Jesus, to drink the cup before us.

Jesus saw God—but then was plunged into darkness. And everyone who follows him into that darkness, into pain or despair, into the apparent abandonment of God, must develop night-vision, to obey when we can't see, to trust when we can't bear it—and yet he enables us. We trust, and then we see. ✍

~ *Day 80* ~

"One thing I ask of the LORD, this is what I seek: that I may dwell in the house of the LORD all the days of my life, to gaze upon the beauty of the LORD and to seek him in his temple."

~ Psalm 27:4

The *Footprints* poem says he is carrying us in the hardest times. To me that used to be a nice sentiment, something that good Christians imagine but not a promise to rest in. When I pray now, I pour out my heart until God says, "Be still, and know that I am God." I used to just stop praying, but now I bask in prayer, knowing that he is God. I rest in his arms because his perfect plan is in action; I am secure in the shelter of his wings. That's when he begins to speak to me. That's when I am filled by him.

I used to be afraid to seek God's presence because I thought, *my faith is too fragile to handle silence. It is better to imagine God than to seek him and be disappointed.* I mistook God's silence for rejection instead of his beckoning call to seek and pursue him, and I missed out on knowing the beauty of when God does answer. A. W. Tozer writes:

"God wills that we should push on into his presence and live our whole lives there...the presence of God is the central fact of Christianity...The type of Christianity which happens now to be the vogue knows this Presence only in theory... According to its teachings we are in the presence of God positionally, and nothing is said about the need to experience that Presence actually...The world is perishing for lack of the knowledge of God and the Church is famishing for want of his presence." [54]

How I hungered for the "manifest presence" of God. Tozer goes on to explain how the Old Testament tabernacle is a beautiful illustration of going from the "wilds of sin into the enjoyed presence of God."[55] There was only one entrance to the tabernacle, which speaks of Christ. Upon entering, the priest offered a sacrifice for sins. Jesus, our high priest has offered this sacrifice once for all. Then, before entering the Holy Place, the priest was required to wash in the laver—as we "wash in the Word" of God. He passed through a veil into the Holy Place, where there was no natural light—the light of the golden candlestick was the only light, as Jesus is our only light. There was the table of shewbread, the Word of God, and the altar of incense, our continual prayers.

Everything in the tabernacle was put there to lead us to God, to reveal the way to Christ. And then we come to the Most Holy Place, the Holy of Holies, where the Presence of God dwells. Only the High Priest could enter this, and only once a year, so great is God's holiness. A veil several inches thick separated the holy place from the Most Holy Place. This veil tore when Christ died, allowing all believers access to the presence of God. This is the place God beckons us to, where we gaze upon his beauty and enjoy the sheltering of his wings.

Sometimes I break down and tell God I don't have the strength to pursue him and that I need him to come meet me where I am. He has always answered that prayer over time, and then calls me again to seek after him. To trust despite my anger, and take refuge despite the questions. To test the bounds of our relationship and find myself firmly within God's protection.

> "You have to come to the place where God is your only light, prayer your only communion, and God your only sustenance, before you can see God. We go through the Holy Place to get to the Most Holy Place. That's the only way."
>
> ~ Pastor Cliff

Lean Back

As I think on what has changed in the last several years for me, it is not merely that I have been through an intense trial. It's that I began seeking God. He was not distancing himself from me; he wanted me to seek him, like the man who found buried treasure in a field and sold all he had to buy it (Matthew 13:44). Seeking God is surrendering all I am and all I have to God.

I treasure the gift God has given me in his presence through this trial. I wish Dave didn't have to suffer, but Dave is God's servant as I am. I know God won't let this be for nothing. So I endeavor with all my might to somehow join God in this goal and refuse to let it be meaningless.

Often we can't change or control the things that happen to us. But God is in the business of redemption and restoration. Life leaves us broken...he makes us whole. He sees our suffering, he weeps with us, and then he beckons, "don't despair." He can bring good out of the worst evil; he can redeem the lost days and the pain.

God longs for us to know Christ more intimately. When we develop "night-vision" during our "dark nights of the soul," we come to know the breadth and depth of his love for us, to sense his presence in our lives every day.

Ask God to change your heart and reveal himself to you in whatever way he chooses through your trial. This has been my continual prayer and God has greatly answered. Joyce Huggett writes, "The secret of true prayer is to place oneself utterly and completely at the disposal of God's Spirit."[56]

He is waiting for you. Beckoning us to put away imagination and experience him who is real. His Word is open, because he is open to you. He waits for you to come, to listen, to bask in his Light, to be awestruck by him. Will you come? ❧

Chapter Thirteen

A TOUCH WITH A PROMISE
Resting in the Everlasting Arms

Thou hast formed us for Thyself,
and our hearts are restless
till they find rest in Thee.[57]

~ St. Augustine

~ *Day 81* ~

"He who dwells in the shelter of the Most High
will rest in the shadow of the Almighty."

~ Ps 91:1

Hell hath no fury like a woman scorned. Or is that a mother scorned? I had only vengeance on my mind! How *dare* that wasp sting my four-year-old? After putting ice on Zach's finger, I searched for an appropriate weapon. Then I remembered our fly swatter, and rushed outside with it.

There was the mock-innocent, perched on the white plastic patio chair, which Zach regretted reaching for. Big, black, and soon to rue the day it was born! It studied the chair with its feelers. I planted my feet and poised for the kill, my arm cautiously rising as if by a helium balloon of adrenaline. But as I swooped down on the evil creature, it made off like a jet. It was gone.

Lyme disease also leaves me with unused adrenaline. I am ready to attack, but always eluded by my villain.

"In his hand is the life of every creature and the breath of all mankind." Job 12:10. Did God turn his back when Dave went to the woods? Did he glance away, distracted by something at the wrong moment? No, we don't face neglect or negligence. God's eye was not wandering but fixed on Dave when that tick came along—that tiny deer tick, the size of the period at the end of this sentence. God had the power to reach down and squash that tick, or make Dave aware of it in time, or inspire it towards a non-human blood-meal, and chose not to instead.

Why God didn't storm down with his heavenly bug-swatter and thunder, "How dare you think of biting my beloved child!" I can't comprehend. Man left that protective cocoon at original sin, and God seems particular about when he chooses to intervene now. And yet...God chose to save us, to call us his own. Why?

I began to read the Psalms for my quiet times, and the idea came to me to keep a journal of God's character and promises. Every time there was a description of who God was, I would write that down. On the facing page, I wrote who I am. I wanted to embrace God, to claim the promises the Psalmist claimed as my faith, and to see the strength of God's character that the Psalmist saw. In response to Psalm 13 I wrote the following, verse by verse:

Who is God? He hides his face—he doesn't always act immediately, but God listens. He lets me wrestle and sorrow and sometimes lose. He is the giver of light, my only and best hope, the Giver of life. His love is unfailing, his salvation brings joy, he is trustworthy. God is good to me.

Who am I? When I feel lost and alone, I pour out my heart to God. I am honest with God. I am heard. I wrestle with my thoughts, I sorrow, I don't always win. I look to God for answers, help, hope. I weigh the consequences and present to God what I see and fear. Despite how bad it looks, I trust in his unfailing love. I rejoice in his salvation, I sing in thankfulness of his goodness.

We are secure within his sovereignty even when we sorrow or wrestle with confusion. When God hides his face. it's not rejection or indifference or abandonment. His promise is true—God who has counted every hair on our heads never takes his eyes off of us. ‮&‬

~ *Day 82* ~

"There remains, then, a Sabbath-rest for the people of God; for anyone who enters God's rest also rests from his own work, just as God did from his."

~ Hebrews 4:9-10

I began to meditate on God's Word. Not just read it, but dwell on it and proclaim my faith through his Word. I made the words *my* words instead of someone else's. *I* trust, *I* hope, *I* look to God. As I sought God as my refuge and protection, sought to be in his presence, sought to embrace his Word as a reality rather than knowledge, my rest and peace deepened.

Journal

Security is knowing that you are in God's hands even if he chooses not to protect you from whatever harm this world can bring on you. That you are safe for eternity. It is a deep trust, peace, that you are safe. God let my world fall apart, and when I submitted I found he was still in control, and submission found peace, and peace found joy. They are companions.

My life has been full of unrest, of questions I cannot answer, and yet, God extends his beautiful rest to me. He, not my circumstances, is my stronghold, shield, refuge and strength. He fills me with his peace, with his Spirit.

Blessed are those who have learned to acclaim you,
who walk in the light of your presence, O LORD.
They rejoice in your name all day long;
they exult in your righteousness.
For you are their glory and strength...

~ Psalm 89:15-16a ❧

~ *Day 83* ~

My people have committed two sins:
They have forsaken me, the spring of living water,
and have dug their own cisterns,
broken cisterns that cannot hold water.

~ Jeremiah 2:13

When I rested in God, he became a "spring of living water" to me. I had lived so much of my life unwittingly ignoring that spring, seeking to dig my own cistern. And it was a broken cistern that could not hold water. But now I thirsted for him, and sought him. My experience was similar to Joyce Huggett's:

> It had never occurred to me that God wanted me to linger in his presence so that he could show me that he delighted in me. Until now, my prayer had been vocal, busy, sometimes manipulative, always achievement-oriented. To kneel at the foot of a cross, allow music to wash over me so that I could 'just be' with God in a stillness which convinced me that 'he is', that 'he is God', was a new experience. But to 'waste time' for God in this way was changing my life, changing my view of God, changing my perception of prayer, changing my understanding of listening to God.[58]

Revel in the great rest and peace God gives to us. He carries us close to his heart, feeds our souls, enables us to stand firm. His promise is true: He gives rest to the weary, he renews our strength, and he rejoices over us with singing.

> "This is what the Sovereign LORD, the Holy One of Israel, says: "In repentance and rest is your salvation, in quietness and trust is your strength, but you would have none of it."

~ Isaiah 30:15 ∽

~ *Day 84* ~

"For God who said, 'Let light shine out of darkness, made his light to shine in our hearts to give
us the light of the knowledge of the glory of God
in the face of Christ. But we have this treasure in
jars of clay to show that this all-surpassing power
is from God and not from us."

~ 2 Corinthians 4:6-7

Resting in God is not easy—we will be hard pressed, per-
plexed, persecuted, and struck down as 2 Corinthians goes on
to say, but we will not lose heart—we will be renewed day by
day.

I can almost feel the dryness of the clay pot and how quickly it would turn to dust under the pressure when hard pressed
on every side. I can feel the cracks give way to an explosive end,
and the sharpness of the remaining shards, tiny pieces of a life
with no hope of restoration. But this is not who we are. We are
filled with the living water of God. We are like new wineskins,
filled with new wine, God's Holy Spirit. That old clay pot is
passing away, the new has come.

"Neither do men pour new wine into old wineskins. If they do, the skins will burst, the wine
will run out and the wineskins will be ruined. No,
they pour new wine into new wineskins, and both
are preserved."

~ Matthew 9:17

We have within us the new wine. The all-surpassing *power*
from God. We are not an old pot, and we are not to dig broken
cisterns. He has made us new in Christ. We are new wineskins,
able to stretch and grow because we are filled with God's Spirit
who renews us day by day. That old wineskin threatening to
burst is not us, and it melts away as we remember again to trust

the God who is both in us and around us, keeping us safe as we go through this trial. He promises he will never leave us or forsake us.

All of us will come through our times of trial because God makes us able, resilient, pliable, if we are willing to walk with him. And when we come through we will be stronger because his love in us will be overflowing. Then grace and thankfulness rejuvenate our veins like water to parched lips, soothing the esophagus with cooling and healing.

Then we can't contain thankfulness, we pour it out from our hands and feet, from the way we walk and talk and act. Our heart is glad. We are renewed, inwardly, day by day. And our troubles truly are light and momentary.

I can see it! But sometimes the weight and length of our troubles overwhelms. When I give in to that weight, I am looking to the old pot and wondering how, how can I make it? Then he reminds me again: I have within me the new wine of the Spirit, renewing me day by day, and my troubles are light if I let him carry them, and momentary if I remember eternity.

> ...our times are in God's hands... Worrying is carrying tomorrow's load with today's strength—carrying two days at once. It is moving into tomorrow ahead of time. Worrying does not empty tomorrow of its sorrow—it empties today of its strength.[59]
>
> ~ Corrie ten Boom

Regret and worry are broken cisterns—but we have a spring of living water! Everything we rely on in this world is a cistern that cracks and leaks, that can't sustain us in our day of need. When famine comes, then we will know the strength of our resources, or their fallibility. We have met power, face to face, and he is our life. Power to transform, redeem, forgive, and to make us holy. What a glorious promise we have *in Christ.* ❧

~ *Day 85* ~

And you also were included in Christ when you heard the word of truth, the gospel of your salvation. Having believed, you were marked in him with a seal, the promised Holy Spirit, who is a deposit guaranteeing our inheritance until the redemption of those who are God's possession—to the praise of his glory.

~ Ephesians 1:13-14

What kind of inheritance can we expect if the Holy Spirit is the deposit? If God's presence within us is the deposit, how rich will our inheritance of fully being in his presence be!

His seal is a "touch with a promise."

The summer I met Dave, we were both counselors at Camp Wonderland. On our last date of the summer, we ended up by the lake holding hands. The mosquitoes ate well that night, but we didn't much care. Then he leaned over and gave me his first, gentle kiss as he said, "I love you." And then he kissed me again a few minutes later and said, "That's a touch with a promise. A promise I intend to keep."

Dave showed me a small part of the intimacy he intended, and the commitment he was offering. How glorious that kiss was, and yet, so small compared with what was to come—the beauty of being one through marriage.

God seals the promise of so much more to come through the deposit of the Holy Spirit *in us*. What kind of union does he intend with us? He calls us his treasured possession, the apple of his eye. He *lavishes* grace on us. His intentions are trustworthy, and his promises beyond what we can imagine.

God is *pleased* with you. The amazing thing is that we have barely begun to explore what God is extending to us now. The future is incomprehensible! ❧

~ *Day 86* ~

> The watchman opens the gate for him, and the sheep listen to his voice. He calls his own sheep by name and leads them out. When he has brought out all his own, he goes on ahead of them, and his sheep follow him because they know his voice.
>
> ~ John 10:3-4

I've never been much of one for New Year's resolutions. Part of the human struggle to follow God is in the way we try to change ourselves. We return to God, convinced that this time we're different, only to find we are still sheep and we still wander.

Maybe instead of mustering all of our strength against our sheepishness, we should embrace the fact that we are sheep. Rest as a lamb in his arms. Learn to listen and follow his voice. Pray for his grace, mercy, and love to seek us when we stray.

And when we find ourselves on that craggy precipice by our own sheepish folly, bleat to again be rescued. We resolve that we will stop being sheep, but God knows we will wander, that we cannot change ourselves. We were never meant to do this work on our own. We focus on trying not to wander, and mistakenly take things into our own hands. By the nature of the task we will stop listening to God—we miss the love and compassion in his tone.

The mark of the sheep is that they know the Shepherd's voice. This should be our goal. To be called by name, known by him, and to follow him. To rely on the promise that he gathers us in his arms and carries us close to his heart (Isaiah 40:11).

> I am the good shepherd; I know my sheep and my sheep know me—just as the Father knows me and I know the Father—and I lay down my life for the sheep.
>
> ~ John 10:14-15 ∞

~ Day 87 ~

The LORD is my shepherd, I shall not be in want.
He makes me lie down in green pastures,
he leads me beside quiet waters,
he restores my soul.

~ Psalm 23:1-3a

A message-board poster noted that caregivers who stay with their spouses are elevated in the minds of others as saints, while those who leave their spouses are considered selfish and inhuman. There is no middle ground for the "well spouse" or other caregiver. While I believe I am a saint by God's proclamation, as are all believers in Christ, I think this kind of elevation is misleading. I find I am still very much a sheep. I have my highs with God, and yet, still am "prone to wander." I embrace John Wyeth's hymn, *Come, Thou Fount of Every Blessing:*

> O to grace how great a debtor
> daily I'm constrained to be!
> Let Thy goodness, like a fetter,
> bind my wandering heart to Thee:
> Prone to wander, Lord, I feel it,
> Prone to leave the God I love:
> Here's my heart, O take and seal it,
> Seal it for Thy courts above.[60]

I have read that sheep won't drink from running water—only still water. By the quiet water, God restores our souls. He leads us there, do we listen and follow? Or are we so busy trying to quench our thirst by running here and there, that we don't hear him drawing us into solitude where he can speak and we can hear him? He whispers, we learn from Elijah. We need to be somewhere that we can hear him whisper his sweet promises in our ears:

We need to find God, and he cannot be found in noise and restlessness. God is the friend of silence. See how in nature—trees, flowers, grass—grow in silence; see the stars, the moon and sun, how they move in silence...the more we receive in silent prayer, the more we can give in our active life. We need silence to be able to touch souls. The essential thing is not what we say, but what God says to us and through us. All our words will be useless unless they come from within—words which do not give the light of Christ increase the darkness.[61]

~ Mother Teresa

Journal

I think how many years I've resolved to do better or be more for God, and how that goal is really secondary to God's purpose for me. What can I give if I am not receiving from him? What can I hope to offer or be? Why run from him and reject his love in favor of what I in my busy-ness can do? I think this year I will hope only to be more like a sheep. To not be so wise as to think I can do things on my own. To learn what his voice sounds like. To be willing to be carried. And to lie down in the meadow in quiet expectation of him, longing for nothing more than a cool breeze and his presence.

The eternal God is your refuge,
and underneath are the everlasting arms.

~ Deuteronomy 33:27a ✍

Lean Back

What has God promised you? Health? Wealth? Comfort? Ease? We get so easily distracted by this world that we miss THE promise. The great one. The great and precious promises. We think something less will satisfy, something temporal will give us joy or happiness, but they are empty pursuits, dead ends, broken cisterns. The precious promise on which all other promises depend, the covenant, the promise Christ gave his life for— is the relationship, the blessed unity, our oneness with him.

God, stir our hearts! Lord, save us, open our eyes to your beauty and love, we are missing it! We adore you in tiny glimpses and then are enticed away by the cheap trinkets of this world. Help us fix our eyes on you, help us hear your passion for us and respond to your love.

Has God been calling you to rest, to the still solitude where you can fully sense his Spirit? He longs for us to bask in his presence, to be filled by him, to know the beauty of his touch and his promise. It's almost unimaginable, the Holy God of the universe, making us holy so we can be with him.

Each day when I get up, I put a ring on my right index finger. That is where a Jewish woman would wear her betrothed's ring. As I slip it on, I hear his tender voice declaring his love anew every day, reminding me of his vows:

Putting on the Promises

I have loved you with an everlasting love.
I will never stop doing good to you.
You are my treasured possession.
I rejoice in doing good to you.
Never will I leave you, never will I forsake you.
I gave my son for you.

You are the apple of my eye.

I rejoice over you with singing!

I'm pleased with you. You make my heart glad.

I am preparing a place for you. I will come back for you.

I will be your shield and strength, your righteousness and reward.

I will rescue and redeem you. We are one.

My eyes are always on you; I've counted every hair on your head.

I am jealous for your love.

You are mine, and I will never let you go.

Let me carry your burdens today.

> "For I know the plans I have for you," declares the LORD, "plans to prosper you and not to harm you, plans to give you hope and a future. Then you will call upon me and come and pray to me, and I will listen to you. You will seek me and find me when you seek me with all your heart. I will be found by you," declares the LORD.
>
> ~Jeremiah 29:11-13.

Listen to the heart of the One who loves you. Carve out some time for quiet, for him. Don't let a hectic life talk you out of it! It may seem awkward at first, but practice, train your ear to listen for him, be patient—and he will reward your endurance.

Psalm 119 reads almost like wedding vows—the author knows the promises, the assurance of God's word so well that he treasures it far above gold or silver and responds with passion. Over and over we read, "according to your promises," and, "according to your word." Meditate on Psalm 119 and ask the Lord to fill your heart with a deeper sense of his love and with passion for him. God has covenanted with us and lavishes grace on us through his great and precious promises. The Bridegroom awaits us. ‌🙠

Chapter Fourteen

APPLE OF HIS EYE
Remembering I Am Precious
When Pain Makes Me Forget

For the LORD's portion is his people, Jacob his allotted inheritance. In a desert land he found him, in a barren and howling waste. He shielded him and cared for him; he guarded him as the apple of his eye...

~ Deuteronomy 32:9-10

~ *Day 88* ~

For the LORD takes delight in his people;
he crowns the humble with salvation.
Let the saints rejoice in this honor
and sing for joy on their beds.

~ Psalm 149:4-5

The words of my four-year-old son still echo in my mind. He answered a foundational question of American society, one we spend a lifetime answering, only to find our answer fails us.

We were getting ready for the cross-country trip to Dave's doctor. The kids were staying with some friends, and Zach had packed his clothes and most precious toys—all except for Cow.

"Cow" as we affectionately called it, always slept with Zach and went everywhere he did. Once, he dropped it by mistake at the Madison, Wisconsin airport. "Would the owner of the black and white cow please come to the information desk?" paged the loudspeaker. A snicker spread like a gentle breeze throughout the gates of waiting passengers. The owner, nestled in his stroller and farm blanket, was not yet two.

"Are you sure you don't want to take Cow?" I asked.

"No," came the sure reply. "Cow's a Home-Rester like Daddy."

I was stunned into silence. Zach had found an answer to the question everyone asks, although I wondered if anyone ever asked him, "What does your Daddy do?" The question where we turn occupation into identity, and work into the measure of man's value. But true value comes not from what we can do, but from the person who chooses to value the relationship. We have value because we belong to God. We are his people.

Keep me as the apple of your eye,
hide me in the shadow of your wings…

~ Psalm 17:8 ⁊

~ *Day 89* ~

For you are a people holy to the LORD your God.
The LORD your God has chosen you out of all the
peoples on the face of the earth to be his people,
his treasured possession.

~ Deuteronomy 7:6

When my grandfather was dying, it didn't reduce his value to me that he could no longer recount all the old stories of his life, his work exploits, or raising my dad and uncle. It didn't matter if he could no longer add six-figure columns faster than a computer or show the bank how they figured his interest incorrectly and owed him another ten cents.

I valued all of these things, but most of all I valued him. He couldn't be reduced to an occupation. His value as "shrewd businessman" was only the tip of the iceberg, and did not reveal his hidden tender side, his joy in giving beautiful things, the look in his eye he saved for his loved ones, or the strength that upheld us when his arm was around us. No title could encompass his value.

As I think about the question, "What do you do," it intrigues me. It's as if we ask someone, "why do you have value?" or "what do you do that's of value?"

Years ago I read about a four-year old boy with Down Syndrome. His mom was with a friend who was struggling with panic attacks. The little boy crawled into her lap and held her for the longest time. It was what she needed. That is his legacy.

One time I heard two women talking about another woman who had given birth to a baby with a severe birth defect. The baby died within several months. "The pregnancy should have been terminated," one said abruptly, never acknowledging that the pregnancy was not just a medical condition, but a process by which God creates a soul-bearing life.

All these thoughts flashed through my mind as Zach's words repeated over and over, "Cow's a Home-Rester, like Daddy." I was stunned into silent agreement that Cow could stay home. I rejoiced in the pride with which it was said, the pride of a son for his father. Zach doesn't yet know that "accomplishment equals value." I hope he never does. We have value because the God of the universe has made us his treasured possession. ∞

~ *Day 90* ~

...I consider everything a loss compared to the
surpassing greatness of knowing Christ Jesus
my Lord, for whose sake I have lost all things.
I consider them rubbish, that I may gain Christ...

~ Philippians 3:8

I am not saying that our desire to accomplish things and be useful does not have merit, or that it's not both terrifying and humiliating to have that ability taken away. But in God's economy, we are all useful and imbued with value.

To define our value by what we do, or our lack of value by what we cannot do, is antithetical to the Christian faith, and misses entirely the Gospel of Christ. It is to elevate our secondary purpose instead of our primary one. We belong to God, not the world, and we are his to do with as he pleases. Our purpose, our productivity, if defined by God, may have a very different meaning than what man deems "productive."

I will never forget my shock at studying Paul's letter to the Philippians. Most important to him was knowing Christ. Not spreading the Gospel (which he greatly valued), but *knowing* Christ.

Billy Graham was once asked in an interview if he would change anything about his life, and he answered that he wished he had spent more time with his family.

When I heard that, the value of my family increased a thousand fold. It was as if God had said that Dave and Zach and Anna were as important to God as the rest of the world. As if being a wife and mother had as much value to God as being Billy Graham. God truly accepted and valued our family.

Disability does not mean one has been thrown away by God. The abilities are different, what one can accomplish may be different—but our value to God is not diminished.

I confess and repent that in my heart I have falsely accused God of having wandering eyes, of not really looking out for us, not really helping us. By contrast, the truth is that we are his temple that he has consecrated, and he has put his Name on us forever.

> My eyes and my heart will always be there.
>
> ~I Kings 9:3

> They will be my people,
> and I will be their God.
>
> ~Jeremiah 32:38

Do you hear his heart? We are *his* and he is *ours*. His covenant is beyond "till death do us part." He will never stop doing good to us. He has not turned away or taken his eyes off of us for an instant. We may not know all his purposes, but he *allures* us, speaks *tenderly* to us, *covenants* with heart and soul, gives all for us…for our good.

> They will be called the Holy People,
> the Redeemed of the LORD;
> and you will be called Sought After,
> the City No Longer Deserted.
>
> —Isaiah 62:12

You are *Sought After*. You have captured his heart and he will not look away. ∞

~ *Day 91* ~

His pleasure is not in the strength of the horse,
nor his delight in the legs of a man;
the LORD delights in those who fear him,
who put their hope in his unfailing love.

~ Psalm 147:10-11

I wonder how many of us grasp the truth that God delights in us. The Bible is full of such verses. God values us and values our sacrifices when we are seeking him. I am not sure why. He doesn't have to. But he chooses to identify with us—we are chosen by him as the bride for his Son. Bask in his love.

If our hope, instead, is in what we do for God—how devastating that hope when old age or disability comes.

I am so blessed to have Dave in my life. He reminds me through his words and actions that when we value what God values, we become conformed to his image.

God values our lives and does not ignore our pain. He collects our tears, every one, in a bottle. He knows what it is to suffer when tempted. He knows what it is to be persecuted. He knows what it is to be obedient to death, and he calls us to be the same. Jesus shows us the way to full and complete obedience to the point of shedding our blood. He never tells us our sacrifices are meaningless, because he himself has taken this very journey. The journey shows the true depth of the value God has assigned to us.

You keep track of all my sorrows.
You have collected all my tears in your bottle.
You have recorded each one in your book.

~ Psalm 56:8, NLT ∞

~ *Day 92* ~

The LORD saw how great man's wickedness on the
earth had become, and that every inclination of
the thoughts of his heart was only evil all the
time. The LORD was grieved that he had made
man on the earth, and his heart was filled with
pain. So the LORD said, I will wipe mankind,
whom I have created, from the face of the earth.

~ Genesis 6:5-7

I am very disturbed when I think about God's grief. When I
started thinking about why God grieved, I wondered why he
didn't wipe us all away. His grief goes down to my very core. It
silences me and shakes me and makes me wonder how he continued on. How did he deal with grief? How did he go from the
grief that made him wish he'd never made man on the earth, to
the joy set before him that led Christ to endure the cross (Hebrews 12:2)?

The joy set before God is, surprisingly, us. When mankind
was useless, completely incapable of fulfilling God's purposes,
God did not throw us away but invested his love in us. God
made a commitment and did not give up on it even though he
was grieved. Despite everything, he delights in us. He has chosen to love us; he wants us!

It is Satan's goal to keep the depth of that truth from us. He
will weigh us down with our own imperfections, with self-
destructive thoughts, with terrible circumstances, with whatever
he can think to bring into our lives—and we help him along.
We continue those thoughts, we cause a lot of those circumstances with hatred, selfishness, gossip, lack of unity, our lack of
responsiveness to God's voice—and all the while God is there,
grieving again over his children (Ephesians 4:30).

Teach us, Lord, how to love you and love your children. Help us see, as you did, the joy set before us in your presence and in your saints.

The choice God made to love carried him from the grief of Genesis 6 to the joy of Hebrews 12. Love is the thread that goes from grief beyond bearing to joy beyond words and sews the garment of humanity together in Christ.

He cherishes us, and we can cherish each other. We can take the thread of love and weave it in and out of the fibers of our relationships until we are attached inextricably one to another, a fabric that is strong and won't tear or snag on life's sharp edges. We are all different, but are called to be his tapestry of love. ❧

~ *Day 93* ~

> Finally, let no one cause me trouble, for I bear on my body the marks of Jesus.
>
> ~ Galatians 6:17

Paul's suffering marked him as a servant of Christ, and in one sense, Dave also bears in his body the marks of Christ. He has not had the privilege of suffering persecution for Christ, and yet God has used his suffering in my life. I never understood my own pride and selfishness until faced with this challenge. I never understood the depth of my self-reliance. And I never understood the depth of God's love, how far his arms reach out to me, how he longs for daily communion with me, until our lives began to fall apart.

Before we were married, Dave always said that he wanted to set me free. I don't think he realized what it would cost him, but through his illness, I am at last free to see God as I have never seen him before. He has helped me "throw off everything that hinders and the sin that so easily entangles" and to "run the race set before us…" (Hebrews 12:1-2).

I am humbled beyond words and hope one day, Dave will understand what a strange and wonderful gift he has given to me and our children. He has truly suffered on our behalf, and for Christ.

> "Therefore, since Christ suffered in his body, arm yourselves also with the same attitude, because he who has suffered in his body is done with sin. As a result, he does not live the rest of his earthly life for evil human desires, but rather for the will of God."
>
> ~ 1 Peter 4:1-2 ✺

~ *Day 94* ~

Ascribe to the LORD, O families of nations,
ascribe to the LORD glory and strength,
ascribe to the LORD the glory due his name.
Bring an offering and come before him;
worship the LORD in the splendor of his holiness.

~ 1 Chronicles 16:28-29

The most precious thing in all of heaven, Jesus' blood, was spilled for us. That's the high price God puts on us. We can't even comprehend that he would give us such a great and undeserved value. He has chosen to love us, and he calls us into a deep relationship, into his Holy of Holies.

There, in the secret room, the Holy of Holies, is his presence, his holiness protected, waiting to be revealed to us. We can't comprehend it in the outer courts or in the world. There it is like a shield. We see his holiness, and we are perhaps blinded by its brilliance, confused by it, discouraged or turned off by it. We don't understand what it means. But in that room, even the name—Holy of Holies—suggests intimacy; he wants to reveal his holiness. To let us in to understand the part of him the world will never know. The veil is torn. He beckons us to come inside. He chooses to dwell within us, and calls the believer his temple.

We know God is pleased with us because he goes with us. This is the culmination of our trials; this is why God would allow us to go through the struggles. God's presence is the prize.

When God invites us into the Holy of Holies, he is extending a trust to us. How can we be worthy of such a trust? We don't have to be worthy—Jesus makes us worthy. We have to be willing. Are we willing to seek him, to trust him as he extends trust to us? He has chosen us for a special revelation of himself that seems to only come through trial and suffering.

God wants to satisfy over-abundantly. If we go to heaven being satisfied with mere comfort and possessions and surroundings—won't he gladly give us all of these? And yet it will be so far short of what could be, what he hopes for, the real joy in store for us. He pours out his love into our hearts. This is the real finale of considering it pure joy. How far short we come if we stop with perseverance or character, or the hope of it all being over some day.

> For Zion's sake I will not keep silent,
> for Jerusalem's sake I will not remain quiet,
> till her righteousness shines out like the dawn,
> her salvation like a blazing torch.
> The nations will see your righteousness,
> and all kings your glory;
> you will be called by a new name
> that the mouth of the LORD will bestow.
> You will be a crown of splendor in the LORD's hand,
> a royal diadem in the hand of your God.
> No longer will they call you Deserted,
> or name your land Desolate.
> But you will be called Hephzibah,
> and your land Beulah;
> for the LORD will take delight in you,
> and your land will be married.
> As a young man marries a maiden,
> so will your sons marry you;
> as a bridegroom rejoices over his bride,
> so will your God rejoice over you.

~ Isaiah 62:1-5 ∾

~ *Day 95* ~

Both the one who makes men holy and those who are made holy are of the same family. So Jesus is not ashamed to call them brothers.

~ Hebrews 2:11

Jesus is not ashamed to call us brothers. "Whoever does the will of my father is my brother and sister and mother" (Matthew 12:50). It is easy to imagine God as our Father—our maker, authority, guide. But Jesus our brother is truly glory for us. I just hope to sit at his feet as Mary did, and listen to him. We have a family identity in Christ, we are his chosen, holy and dearly loved.

Journal

> *Be Still*
>
> *God called me tonight.*
> *He wanted just to be with me*
> *In beautiful, silent communion.*
> *Not to give me a job*
> *Or something to learn,*
> *Just to be.*
> *Be still and know that I am God.*
> *Drink him in and be filled and fulfilled.*
> *Be still and know me.*
>
> *I long for intimacy and oneness with you.*
> *Be still.*
> *Tonight there are no questions,*
> *No agendas, no lists.*
> *Tonight I did not summon God.*
> *Tonight he summoned me*
> *Just to be*
> *In silent, intimate communion with him.*
> *Be still, and know that I am God.*

Fear not, for I have redeemed you;
I have summoned you by name; you are mine.
When you pass through the waters, I will be with you;
and when you pass through the rivers,
they will not sweep over you.
When you walk through the fire, you will not be burned;
the flames will not set you ablaze.

~ Isaiah 43:1b-2 ∽

Lean Back

...Then he appeared and the soul felt its worth...

~ O Holy Night

Do you feel your worth? The God of the universe delights in us—this truth is amazing. Go to him today and let God remind you again that you are precious to him, the apple of his eye, his beloved.

> "For he says, "In the time of my favor I heard you, and in the day of salvation I helped you." I tell you, now is the time of God's favor, now is the day of salvation."

~ 2 Corinthians 6:2

You are his portion, his inheritance, and now is the time of his favor. You are his temple. "If anyone destroys God's temple, God will destroy him; for God's temple is sacred, and you are that temple." (1 Corinthians 3:17).

This is why Jesus struck Saul with a bright light when Saul persecuted the church, and said, "Saul, Saul, why are you persecuting me?" We and Christ are one, and our persecution is his. We are glued to him, implanted in the vine, married, members of the same body. A father chooses a bride for his son, and the Lord chooses us to be "in Christ."

When I realize the full truth of our union, I am...shocked, excited, amazed, silenced, horrified, humbled, convicted, awed, undone...loved. Even if we don't realize the reality of this union through every pain—it is, none-the-less, real. ❧

Chapter Fifteen

TASTE AND SEE
That the Lord Is Good

Taste and see that the LORD is good;
blessed is the man who takes refuge in him."

~ Psalm 34:8

~ *Day 96* ~

Like newborn babies, crave pure spiritual milk,
so that by it you may grow up in your salvation,
now that you have tasted that the Lord is good.

~ 1 Peter 2:2-3

When Zach was four, he saw a picture of Jesus with nail prints in his hands. "Mommy, that makes me sad," he kept saying. He was overwhelmed by the thought that Jesus had holes, and he knew they hurt. The eyes of a child. So simple, so beautiful. We worry about so many things. But already Zach knew there should not be holes. There was something in the way he said it that encouraged me to linger. Zach was mourning with God in his four-year-old way: already Christ's love was filling his heart. Already the Gospel was feeding his soul.

We crave hope, we long for joy, we hunger for God…and he urges us to come. Come to the Bread of Life who nourishes our souls. Feed on his Word regularly, day and night, for we are not satisfied with only occasional feedings.

How sweet are your words to my taste,
sweeter than honey to my mouth!

~ Psalm 119:103 ∞

~ *Day 97* ~

> "The days are coming," declares the Sovereign
> LORD, "when I will send a famine through the
> land—not a famine of food or a thirst for water,
> but a famine of hearing the words of the LORD."

~Amos 8:11

"I have a dream, Mommy," Zach confided to me one night when he was six.

"What's your dream, honey?"

"I hope that one day Daddy wakes up and doesn't take his pills, and I'll ask why, and he'll say he's all better."

"I hope for that too, Zach."

Dave took over 50 pills each day back then. "The medicine makes Daddy better," Anna proclaimed. Her unwavering belief in the power of pills was a peculiar curiosity to me since Dave's progress was painstakingly slow.

Oh Zach and Anna! How can I convey to you that God is real, that he's good, that he loves you? You believe me so easily now, but as you grow I know your hungering hearts will doubt and search and question this God who has allowed such pain in our family. And I only pray God will hold you and not let you stray.

So often I have thought, *God, why?* If it was just me, I could make it through this, but my children? And what about Dave—he suffers so much more than I do because of the physical pain on top of the emotional and spiritual anguish. The pain is like a famine, like the darkest wilderness—why does God hide his face?

> A voice of one calling:
> "In the desert prepare the way for the LORD;
> make straight in the wilderness a highway for our God."

~ Isaiah 40:3

Like those who lived through the great famine that Amos prophesied, the 400 years between Malachi and the coming of Christ, we hunger for a word from God. C. S. Lewis said pain is God's megaphone. What is God saying? I pour out my anguish again to him in this desert life we live. But then I remember the voice, crying out in the wilderness. "Prepare the way of the Lord." It is the voice proclaiming a loving God, the One who has not abandoned us, the One who indeed "remembers us" in our desert, and readies us for his presence, our inheritance.

> "And I heard a loud voice from the throne saying, "Now the dwelling of God is with men, and he will live with them. They will be his people, and God himself will be with them and be their God. He will wipe every tear from their eyes. There will be no more death or mourning or crying or pain, for the old order of things has passed away."
>
> ~ Revelation 21:3-4 ∞

~ *Day 98* ~

In his great mercy he has given us new birth into
a living hope through the resurrection of Jesus
Christ from the dead, and into an inheritance that
can never perish, spoil or fade...

~ 1 Peter 1:3-4

I can hardly comprehend that word, inheritance. It seems everywhere I go I hear what I should be doing, what things good Christians do. Sometimes the Christian life seems to me as driven as the rest of the world. There is no rest until I come to that word, *inheritance.*

There is a time for everything. A time to mourn and a time to heal. If I were slave to any other master, I might not have that time—but God has appointed a time for me to heal. A time to work, and a time to rest. A time to build—and a time to tear down. I didn't realize we were in a time to tear down. The tearing down of our dreams and lives, the tearing down of our savings and future. But there will again be a time to build. I don't know exactly when or how. But I know in our future is the inheritance.

Glory in his holy name;
let the hearts of those who seek the LORD rejoice.
Look to the LORD and his strength;
seek his face always.

~ Psalm 105:3-4

The world and its demands can exhaust us. The message some churches proclaim can exhaust us. Then we need to go back to our first purpose of worshiping God. Rejoice when we seek his face, glory in his holy name, look to him—and his strength, not our own. Enjoy choice morsels from his Word; let our souls feast on his love for us.

Do not work for food that spoils, but for food that
endures to eternal life, which the Son of Man will
give you. For on him God the Father has placed
his seal of approval.

~John 6:27

Are you exhausted? God calls to us and offers himself, a
beautiful inheritance. Our job is to go to him when we're hungry, seek his face, and hang onto our faith. We have to let go of
the other voices.

The heavens declare the glory of God;
the skies proclaim the work of his hands.
Day after day they pour forth speech;
night after night they display knowledge.
There is no speech or language
where their voice is not heard.

~ Psalm 19:1-3

~ Day 99 ~

"I am to be the only inheritance the priests have.
You are to give them no possession in Israel; I
will be their possession."

~ Ezekiel 44:28

When God gave the Promised Land over to the Israelites,
he apportioned the land to eleven of the twelve tribes. The
Levitical tribe received no land; the Lord was to be their inheritance, their portion. They served in the tabernacle, later the
temple, and from them the priests were chosen. Now, the believer carries on the priesthood (1 Peter 2:9), and we are his
temple, and God is our portion.

Do we think of God as our inheritance? Do we know who
it is we've inherited? We can spend eternity, and better than the
best book he will keep unfolding, keep revealing himself to us
in deeper and deeper ways. "The LORD confides in those who
fear him" (Psalm 25:14). Confides! Can you believe the intimacy?

I used to read the lists of "Who I am in Christ," and they
never made sense. I rejoiced at first but it "didn't take." It was
as if there was still a veil between me and the gifts, something
still holding them just out of hand's reach.

The gifts will never mean anything until we know the Giver.
I thought I knew Jesus—he had saved me, and I was ready to
move on, "okay, what else is there?" But Jesus IS what else
there is. He is the beginning, middle, and end of our faith journey, *in him* is the joy. We don't move beyond him.

I had so reduced Jesus in my mind to a one-dimensional
concept that I had lost all touch with knowing him at all. I
thought after salvation that my job was to not need him—to

never sin so that I wouldn't need forgiveness, to be righteous on my own. I had a very lonely faith.

But he is the vine and we are the branches—ever needing to feed on his life-giving sap.

Have you ever been around someone truly consumed with love for Jesus while you felt empty? It's like going to a buffet and seeing their plate filled with rich, sumptuous food, while yours has paltry fare. You might think, "I didn't see *that* when I went through the line! I saw some nice table decorations but you have found delicious food." Jesus said,

"My flesh is real food and my blood is real drink."

~John 6:55

He doesn't intend for us to go hungry, to miss out on his riches and abundance. We have tasted the bitter cup, but he has drunk the cup of suffering and wrath to the dregs and drained it dry. We may know well the bitter cup, but Jesus offers another cup at the Lord's Table that satisfies and gives us hope.

We come empty, with only our sin and repentance, with hunger, famished for his love and presence in our lives. Jesus meets us and once again professes his undying love as he offers his body and feeds us with the bread of life and the cup. "Drink from it, all of you," he beckons. Drink in deep draughts of his grace, forgiveness, mercy, and love in abundance. Know intimately the one who has passionately sought after you, who laid down his life *for you.* ❧

~ *Day 100* ~

The Spirit and the bride say, "Come!" And let him who hears say, "Come!" Whoever is thirsty, let him come; and whoever wishes, let him take the free gift of the water of life."

~ Revelation 22:17

Can we say with the Psalmist that we are upright, without flinching? And yet, we are pillars of the tabernacle. We hold up the pure white linen of Christ's righteousness, we stand in our wooden humanity on the brass base of judgment, and are crowned with the silver cap of grace and redemption. We are clothed with Christ in glowing white. Our righteous acts are the fruit of his Spirit and flow from him. He crowns us with redemption—he treats us like royalty.

As I meditate on God's sovereignty and holiness, I am awed at the attention he lavishes on us. Just being on the outskirts of the tabernacle I am overcome by his holiness. And imagine, we enter the Holy of Holies! Just being in proximity to God elicits praise and glory. He is worthy.

John Piper, in his book *Desiring God*, talks about the purpose of man. Slightly altering the Westminster Catechism, he says man's purpose is to "glorify God *by* enjoying him forever."[62]

My daughter Anna at three and a half seemed to have a grasp on this already. One day we were talking about Jesus and she said, "Yeah, he's broken. He got fixed. He's my favorite."

Our problem isn't that we seek pleasure, but that we don't seek pleasure enough—we are satisfied with too little. Is Jesus our favorite? We are satisfied with things that truly don't please, that leave us empty and hollow, with things that don't and can't fill us. *Taste and see,* he beckons us.

I have read that many Americans don't drink enough water. I'm coming to see that our spiritual dehydration is great as well. We deny ourselves because we believe pleasure-seeking is wrong, when perhaps it is our greatest calling.

For me, the greatest spiritual truth I have learned in years is that God can be enjoyed. May we plumb the depths of that truth!

One day I had a vision of a well, and I remembered the scripture that says we will never thirst again, and I reflected on how I just need to drink him in. When I am angry and frustrated and lonely and upset, instead of trying to somehow become more patient magically on my own, I need to see I'm really thirsty, I need him. I need his life in me and filling me. I don't need to draw patience from within me, I need my soul to go to him and "delight in the richest of fare."

Come, all you who are thirsty,
come to the waters;
and you who have no money,
come, buy and eat!
Come, buy wine and milk
without money and without cost.
Why spend money on what is not bread,
and your labor on what does not satisfy?
Listen, listen to me and eat what is good,
and your soul will delight in the richest of fare.

~ Isaiah 55:1-2 ఴ

~ *Day 101* ~

I suggest there are...only two joys. One is having God answer all your prayers; the other is not receiving the answer to all your prayers. I believe this because I have found that God knows my needs infinitely better than I know them. And He is utterly dependable, no matter which direction our circumstances take us.[63]

~ Joni Eareckson Tada

It is such a paradox to rejoice in the eternal and cry over the here and now. I am torn continually from one end of emotion to another, and hope that the struggle will cease, but hope more that I will find strength and courage and joy to make it through.

I can *feel* that God is doing nothing but must go on in the knowledge that God is really there despite my feelings because in my head I know he is. He is "utterly dependable."

We are not abandoned, crushed, destroyed, or despairing, though we are pressed on every side, confused, beaten down and persecuted. We serve a great God, we belong to a great God, and we are in his hands. After we pray and do everything, we have to trust in him for whatever he allows to happen.

"Though the mountains be shaken
and the hills be removed,
yet my unfailing love for you will not be shaken
nor my covenant of peace removed,"
says the LORD, who has compassion on you.

~Isaiah 54:10

This is the great promise we feast on daily until that greatest of all feasts in eternity...the great wedding feast of the Lamb. Today the appetizers...tomorrow the feast! ✍

Lean Back

How lovely is your dwelling place, O LORD Almighty!
My soul yearns, even faints,
for the courts of the LORD;
my heart and my flesh cry out for the living God.
Even the sparrow has found a home,
and the swallow a nest for herself,
where she may have her young—
a place near your altar, O LORD Almighty,
my King and my God.

~ Psalm 84:1-3

Journal

I sit on the river bank, watching the effervescent blue-green tails of dragonflies wave from between jet-black wings, flitting and playing their giddy game of tag. Then they alight and rest, taking a long, slow draught of air as slowly their wings open. Suddenly, as if driven by a spring-loaded mechanism, their wings snap shut again. This is a place where quiet fills the soul.

Silence is that beautiful place where you say, "God, I want you to have all of me," and you hear him say, "I want you to have all of me." Food for the soul.

The waters provide a balm for me as I retrace the steps of my life. Thirteen years of disability God has brought us through so far. Gone are the days when the children were young and I could try to shield them...but God's truth does a much better job of that than I ever could.

This water is murky. I used to see so clearly through the crisp waters of Catfish Creek where I grew up. I remember going on a walk with my friend Rhoda in 6th grade. We were several miles away, but she said we could follow the creek to my house. I was so scared. This didn't look like my creek—it looked more like the small river I am looking at now, and it was so far from home. It did eventually take me home, as I hope this one will too. Home to the place where God is always there.

Blessed are those who dwell in your house;
they are ever praising you. *Selah*
Blessed are those whose strength is in you,
who have set their hearts on pilgrimage.
As they pass through the Valley of Baca,
they make it a place of springs;
the autumn rains also cover it with pools.
They go from strength to strength,
till each appears before God in Zion.

~ Psalm 84:4-7

The pilgrimage, literally, the "highways" in our hearts. Is my mind fixed on pilgrimage? Do all the paths I desire lead to God's holy and awesome presence? Does my heart wander from the God I love?

I lay on my back and look up into the layers of leaves reaching toward the sky. Small and big ones, pointed and smooth, pale and rich, bright, and dark. The reflected sunlight from the water dances on the bottoms of the leaves. God reminds me how I enjoyed a walk in the sun yesterday, when I reveled in its gentle warmth. And God said, "Wait until you revel in my Son tomorrow." "Taste and see that the LORD is good," (Psalm 34:8).

The reflected sunlight strums the leaves like a harp. The Son makes such music in my heart. The symphony of God's presence. I hum Michael W. Smith's Move in Me.

I tried to explain to Anna what it's like to play in a symphony. As incredible as it is to play one instrument and make music, to become part of something bigger, a symphony, is breathtaking. There is a power that's indescribable.

Sometimes in our lives we only hear the harmony, that sad and dissonant tone that hangs onto nothing, lost, forlorn, abandoned. It is the desert, the Baca that we wallow in. Then he calls us and saves us, teaches us to set our hearts on pilgrimage. He shows how to make highways in our minds that lead to him. He shows us our true hunger and is not willing to let us die of thirst in the desert. He holds out so much more to us.

"Your love, O LORD, reaches to the heavens,
your faithfulness to the skies.
Your righteousness is like the mighty mountains,
your justice like the great deep.
O LORD, you preserve both man and beast.
How priceless is your unfailing love!
Both high and low among men
find refuge in the shadow of your wings.
They feast on the abundance of your house;
you give them drink from your river of delights.
For with you is the fountain of life;
in your light we see light."

~ Psalm 36:5-9

Do we see how he cherishes us? Do we feast on the abundance of his house? Do we delight in him, in his kisses and touch, in the shelter of his wings, in his river of delights?

"It's really true," God beckons to us. "Better is one day in my courts than a thousand elsewhere," (Psalm 84:10). "Come, spend some time with me, and together we will make your Baca a place of springs."

*The purpose of man is to glorify God
and enjoy him forever.*[64]
Selah ℘

APPENDIX A

Truth and Lies Chart

Note: This is my lies and truth chart. I include it in case it might help or encourage you. These are not the only lies and truths to be found, but they are a starting place. May God bring you peace and love and comfort through knowing him better.

Lies	Truth
I am unworthy of God's touch and love.	He quiets me with his love—Zephaniah 3:17 He gathers the lambs in his arms and holds them close to his heart—Isaiah 40:11 The one the LORD loves rests between his shoulders—Deuteronomy 33:12
God reluctantly accepts me—only for the sake of his name (So God isn't a liar)	Christ accepts me to God's glory—Romans 15:7 God delights in me, rejoices over me with singing—Zephaniah 3:17 He yearns for me—Jeremiah 31:20 He searches for me when I'm lost—Ezekiel 34:11-16
God made a mistake in choosing me, He regrets that choice.	"In him we have redemption through his blood, the forgiveness of sins, in accordance with the riches of God's grace that he lavished on us with all wisdom and understanding."—Ephesians 1:7-8

God may forgive, but begrudgingly. He does not sympathize. I can't go to him	"For we do not have a High Priest who is unable to sympathize with our weaknesses, but we have one who has been tempted in every way, just as we are, yet was without sin. Let us approach the throne of grace with confidence, so that we may receive mercy and find grace to help us in our time of need." —Hebrews 4:14-16
I can't be like Jesus. I can't bear his image	"And we, who with unveiled faces all reflect the Lord's glory, are being transformed into his likeness with ever-increasing glory, which comes from the Lord, who is the Spirit." —2 Corinthians 3:18
I'm on my own to try to please God.	God's intention is to present me to himself, holy and blameless, thru Christ. —Ephesians 5:27, Colossians 1:22, 28
God abandons us when we're hurting	The LORD is close to the brokenhearted and saves those who are crushed in spirit. —Psalm 34:18
I have no value	I am made in God's image —Genesis 1:26
I am not safe.	"The LORD is my rock, my fortress and my deliverer in whom I take refuge. He is my shield and the horn of my salvation, my stronghold."—Psalm 18:2 "Because of the LORD's great love, we are not consumed." —Lamentations 3:22

God detests me.	"He rescued me because he delighted in me." —Psalm 18:19
God abandons me	"Be content with such things as you have because God has said, 'never will I leave you, never will I forsake you.'" —Hebrews 13:5
I have no value or significance to God	"Fear not, for I have redeemed you; I have summoned you by name; you are mine. When you pass through the waters, I will be with you…Since you are precious and honored in my sight, and because I love you, I will give men in exchange for you, and people in exchange for your life." —Isaiah 43:1-2, 4
Love is never free, it always has strings attached.	"Come, all you who are thirsty, come to the waters; and you who have no money, come, buy and eat! Come, buy wine and milk without money and without cost. Why spend money on what is not bread, and your labor on what does not satisfy? Listen, listen to me, and eat what is good, and your soul will delight in the richest of fare." —Isaiah 55:1-2
God doesn't forgive	If we confess our sins, he is faithful and just to forgive our sins and purify us from all unrighteousness. —I John 1:9
God isn't pleased with my performance	God doesn't count our sins against us. Blessed is the one whose sins are not counted against him. —1 Corinthians 5:17-21 Romans 4:7

God is harsh and demanding	"He tends his flock like a shepherd: he gathers the lambs in his arms and carries them close to his heart; he gently leads those that have young." —Isaiah 40:11
	"Take my yoke upon you and learn from me, for I am gentle and humble in heart, and you will find rest for your souls. For my yoke is easy and my burden is light." —Matthew 11:29-30
God isn't dependable. God isn't reliable	"Yet this I call to mind and therefore I have hope: Because of the LORD's great love we are not consumed, for his compassions never fail. They are new every morning; great is your faithfulness." —Lamentations 3:21-23
	"What if some did not have faith? Will their lack of faith nullify God's faithfulness? Not at all! Let God be true, and every man a liar." —Romans 3:3-4
	"A bruised reed he will not break, and a smoldering wick he will not snuff out. In faithfulness he will bring forth justice;" —Isaiah 42:3
God's love is conditional	God loved me when I was a sinner, before I was saved—Romans 5:8. If He loved me while an enemy, now that I'm his child my sin can't change that love.
	His love never changes, never fails: "'Though the mountains be shaken and the hills be removed, yet my unfailing love for you will not

be shaken nor my covenant of peace be removed,' says the LORD, who has compassion on you." —Isaiah 54:10

Shame, hopeless that I'll ever change	"And we, who with unveiled faces all reflect the Lord's glory, are being transformed into his likeness with ever-increasing glory, which comes from the Lord, who is the Spirit" —2 Corinthians 3:18
I can't fight all these thoughts. There are too many.	"'No weapon forged against you will prevail, and you will refute every tongue that accuses you. This is the heritage of the servants of the LORD, and this is their vindication from me,' declares the LORD." —Isaiah 54:17

Stand Firm: —Exodus 14:13, 1 Corinthians 16:13, Ephesians 6:10-18
"In addition to all this, take up the shield of faith, with which you can extinguish all the flaming arrows of the evil one."
—Ephesians 6:16

"Now it is God who makes both us and you stand firm in Christ." —2 Corinthians 1:21

I can't please God	**I can please him in every way:** "For this reason, since the day we heard about you, we have not stopped praying for you and asking God to fill you with the knowledge of his will through all spiritual wisdom and understanding. And we pray this in order that you may live a life worthy of the Lord and may please him in every way: bearing fruit in

every good work, growing in the knowledge of God, being strengthened with all power according to his glorious might so that you may have great endurance and patience, and joyfully giving thanks to the Father, who has qualified you to share in the inheritance of the saints in the kingdom of light."
—Colossians 1:9-12

I can receive a rich welcome into heaven: "For this very reason, make every effort to add to your faith goodness; and to goodness, knowledge; and to knowledge, self-control; and to self-control, perseverance; and to perseverance, godliness; and to godliness, brotherly kindness; and to brotherly kindness, love. For if you possess these qualities in increasing measure, they will keep you from being ineffective and unproductive in your knowledge of our Lord Jesus Christ. But if anyone does not have them, he is nearsighted and blind, and has forgotten that he has been cleansed from his past sins. Therefore, my brothers, be all the more eager to make your calling and election sure. For if you do these things, you will never fall, and you will receive a rich welcome into the eternal kingdom of our Lord and Savior Jesus Christ." —2 Peter 1:5-11

APPENDIX B

Caregiver Checklist

Beloved Caregiver,

The God of the universe, a holy God full of glory, has a plan for each one of us, and right now his plan for you includes caring for your loved one. It is a holy task, and he has counted you worthy of living for someone for whom Christ spilled his precious blood. To do this task, you also need to take care of yourself.

- ❖ Are you eating nutritious food?
- ❖ Drinking plenty of water?
- ❖ Getting enough sleep at night?
- ❖ Resting when you need to?
- ❖ Refreshing yourself in God's Word?
- ❖ Being honest with God?
- ❖ Getting fresh air and sunshine?
- ❖ Exercising, taking walks?
- ❖ Seeking Wise Counsel?
- ❖ Getting time with friends?
- ❖ Making your marriage a priority?
- ❖ Getting time to recharge?
- ❖ Letting others meet your needs?
- ❖ Putting the outcome in God's hands?

> Come to me, all you who are weary and burdened, and I will give you rest. Take my yoke upon you and learn from me, for I am gentle and humble in heart, and you will find rest for your souls. For my yoke is easy and my burden is light.
>
> Matthew 11:28-30 ❧

END NOTES

Chapter 1-Eyes That Behold Him

[1] Helen Keller (1880-1968). BrainyQuote.com, *Xplore Inc*, 2011. http://www.brainyquote.com/quotes/quotes/h/helenkelle114881.html, accessed February 2, 2013.

[2] *Chronic Care in America: A 21st Century Challenge, a study of the Robert Wood Johnson Foundation & Partnership for Solutions:* Johns Hopkins University, Baltimore, MD for the Robert Wood Johnson Foundation (September 2004 Update). "Chronic Conditions: Making the Case for Ongoing Care." As referenced in the "Fact Sheet and Statistics About Chronic Illness," *Rest Ministries*, 2008. http://www.restministries.org/invisibleillness/statistics.htm accessed February 2, 2013.

[3] U.S. Department of Commerce (1994). Bureau of the Census, Statistical Brief: *Americans With Disabilities.* (Publication SB/94-1).U.S. Department of Commerce (1997). Bureau of the Census, Census Brief: *Disabilities Affect One-Fifth of All Americans.* (Publication CENBR/97-5).

U.S. Department of Commerce (1997). Census Bureau*: Current Population Reports.* (Publication P70-61). Author: John McNeill, *Rest Ministries*, 2008.

[4] Kenneth Baker, General Editor, Donald Burdick, John Stek, Walter Wessel, Ronald Youngblood, Associate Editors. *NIV Study Bible.* (Grand Rapids: Zondervan, 1995), Matthew 27:46

[5] Colin Welland. *Chariots of Fire.* Film. Directed by Hugh Hudson. Great Britain: David Puttnam, 1981.

[6] *Chronic Care in America: A 21st Century Challenge, a study of the Robert Wood Johnson Foundation. Rest Ministries*, 2008.

[7] National Health Interview Survey (n.d.). *Rest Ministries*, 2008.

[8] Mackenzie TB, Popkin MK: *Suicide in the medical patient*, Intl J Psych in Med 17:3-22, 1987. *Rest Ministries*, 2008.

[9] John Piper, *A Hunger for God* , (Wheaton: Crossway Books, 1997), 11.

John Piper, *Desiring God: Meditations of a Christian Hedonist, 10th Anniversary Expanded Edition* (Sisters: Multnomah Books, 1996), 50.

[10] Edward Pearse, *The Best Match* or *The Soul's Espousal to Christ* (Morgan, PA: Soli Deo Gloria Publications, 1994), 145

[11] Isaac Watts, "When I Survey the Wondrous Cross," *Hymns and Spiritual Songs* (1707)

Chapter 2-Call Me Mara

[12] Warren W. Wiersbe, *Why Us? When Bad Things Happen to God's People* (Old Tappan, N.J.: Fleming H. Revell, 1984), 27

[13] Charles R. Swindoll, *Laugh Again: Experience Outrageous Joy* (Dallas: Word Publishing, 1992), 34

[14] Jim Cymbala, *Fresh Wind Fresh Fire: What Happens When God's Spirit Invades the Heart of His People* (Grand Rapids: Zondervan, 1997), 159

[15] Charles Swindoll, *Job: A Man of Heroic Endurance-Great Lives Series* (Nashville: Thomas Nelson-W, 2004),15

[16] 2 Cor. 12:7-10

[17] Nowakowski J, Schwartz I, Liveris D, Wang G, Aguero-Rosenfeld ME, Girao G, McKenna D, Nadelman RB, Cavaliere LF, Wormser GP. *Laboratory diagnostic techniques for patients with early Lyme disease associated with erythema migrans: a comparison of different techniques.* Abstract. http://www.ncbi.nlm.nih.gov/pubmed/11700579 accessed February 2, 2013.

Two common reasons for false negative results are testing too early, and low antibodies due to antibiotic use after the initial infection: http://www.cdc.gov/lyme/faq/index.html#accurate accessed February 2, 2013.

"Lyme Borreliosis (LB) is diagnosed clinically, as no currently available test, no matter the source or type, is definitive in ruling in or ruling out infection with these pathogens..." Joseph J. Burrascano Jr., MD. *Advanced Topics in Lyme Disease: Diagnostic Hints and Treatment Guidelines for Lyme and Other Tick Borne Illnesses.* Fifteenth Edition, Copyright September, 2005. http://www.ilads.org/files/burrascano_0905.pdf accessed February 2, 2013.

The CDC says that diagnosis should be based on signs and symptoms and possible exposure to ticks. http://www.cdc.gov/lyme/diagnosistesting/index.html accessed February 2, 2013.

International Lyme and Associated Diseases Society's Position Paper: their view is that the CDC guidelines are an oversimplification of a complex issue. http://www.ilads.org/about_ILADS/position_papers3.html accessed February 2, 2013.

[18] Genesis 32:24-30

[19] Robert S. McGee, *The Search for Significance: Seeing Your True Worth through God's Eyes.* (Nashville: W Publishing Group,2003), 156

Chapter 5-Good Medicine

[20] Betsy George, received via email June 6, 2008

Part 2-Character and Hope

[21] Helen Keller, Jack Belck editor, *The Faith of Helen Keller*. (Hallmark Cards, Inc; First Edition, 1967), back cover

Chapter 6-Who Is God?

[22] R. C. Sproule, *Surprised by Suffering*. (Wheaton: Tyndale House, 1989), 53

[23] Genesis 15

[24] Genesis 9:12-17

[25] Job 42:7-8

[26] Kevin DeYoung, *The Good News We Almost Forgot: Rediscovering the Gospel in a 16th Century Catechism* (Chicago: Moody, 2010), 57

[27] Dunn, 30

[28] A. W. Tozer, *The Pursuit of God: The Human Thirst for the Divine*, (Camp Hill, PA: Christian Publications, 1982, 1993), 83

Chapter 7-Fighting the Battles

[29] The Rule of St. Benedict, Prologue, verse 41

[30] Ronald Dunn, *When Heaven is Silent: Live by Faith, Not by Sight*, (Nashville: Thomas Nelson, 1994), 38

[31] Wiersbe, 109-110

[32] Dunn, 36

Chapter 8- "Snakes in My Veins"

[33] Corrie ten Boom, *He Cares, He Comforts: In Sickness and in Health*, (Old Tappan, N.J. : Fleming H Revell, 1977), 25-26

[34] Florence Nightengale, *Notes on Nursing: What it is and What it is Not*, (London: Harrison, 1859), 35

[35] Wiersbe, 41

Chapter 9-Breaking Pride's Image

[36] Mother Teresa, 1910-1997

[37] Gordon MacDonald, *Ordering Your Private World, Expanded Edition*, (Nashville: Oliver-Nelson, a division of Thomas Nelson Publishers, 1985), chapters 4 and 5.

[38] Piper, *Desiring God*, 85

Chapter 10-God, How Much More?

[39] The American Heritage Dictionary, Second College Edition (Boston: Houghton Mifflin Company, 1985), 449, 140

[40] DeYoung, 89

Part 3-God Pours Out His Love

[41] Larry Crabb, *The Safest Place on Earth: Where People Connect and are Forever Changed,* (Nashville: Thomas Nelson-W Publishing Group, 1999), 39

Chapter 11-The Joy of Submission

[42] John 17:11

[43] Romans 8:31-39

Chapter 12-Awestruck by His Presence

[44] Philip Yancey, "National Tragedy and the Empty Tomb" *Christianity Today* April 2013: 27. Print.

[45] Joyce Huggett, *The Joy of Listening to God: Hearing the Many Ways God Speaks to Us*, (Downers Grove: InterVarsity Press, 1986), pg. 124

[46] Yancey, *Christianity Today*: 28

[47] Edward Mote, *The Solid Rock*, *circa* 1834; first appeared in Mote's *Hymns of Praise*, 1836.

[48] Cymbala, 28, 58

[49] Thomas P. McDonnell, Editor, *A Thomas Merton Reader*, *Revised Edition* (New York: Doubleday Image, 1974), 40, excerpt from *Passage*

[50] Joni Eareckson Tada, *Secret Strength: For Those Who Search,* (Portland: Multnomah, 1988), 14

[51] Doris Van Stone, *No Place To Cry* (Chicago: Moody, 1990) as referenced in Jerry B. Jenkins, Editor, *Families*: *Practical Advice From More Than 50 Experts,* (Chicago: Moody Press, 1993), 162

[52] Ken Gire, The North Face of God: *Hope for the Times When God Seems Indifferent* (Carol Stream: Tyndale House, 2005), 144

[53] Luke 22:43

[54] Tozer, chapter 3

[55] Tozer, chapter 3

[56] Huggett, 54

Chapter 13-A Touch with a Promise

[57] St. Augustine, *Confessions*, c. 397, as seen in Tozer, 31.

[58] Huggett, Pg. 34

[59] ten Boom, 83

[60] John Wyeth (1770-1858), *Come Thou Fount of Every Blessing*

[61] Malcolm Muggeridge, Something Beautiful for God (Garden City, N.Y.: Image, 1977), 48, as referenced in MacDonald, 127

Chapter 15-Taste and See

[62] Piper, *Desiring God*, 15

[63] Joni Eareckson (Tada), *Joni: The Unforgettable Story of a Young Woman's Struggle Against Quadriplegia and Depression*, (Minneapolis: World Wide Publications, 1976), Preface

[64] *Westminster Shorter Catechism*, Question 1.

To order, please visit our website:

HOPE IS MY ANCHOR
www.hopeismyanchor.com

In the US, send $14.95 plus $4 shipping and handling to the address below. Illinois Residents add 6.25% tax ($.93 each).

Merry Marinello
Hope Is My Anchor
134 N. Mernitz Ave.
Freeport, IL 61032

Foreign customers, please contact us
for shipping information.

CPSIA information can be obtained
at www.ICGtesting.com
Printed in the USA
FFOW03n1749120214
3578FF